How to Run Better Business Meetings

A Businessman's Guide to Meetings That Get Things Done

By B. Y. Auger

VISUAL PRODUCTS DIVISION, 3M COMPANY, ST. PAUL, MINNESOTA

©MINNESOTA MINING AND MANUFACTURING COMPANY 1972
Library of Congress Catalog Card Number 66-24061
Printed in the United States of America

Foreword

Communication.

How often do we hear the plea for the need of it and how often the lament about the lack of it?

No one likes to be in the dark about where he is going and how to get there. Picture a venture into space in which those involved are uncertain about their destination and how to achieve it.

The same applies to companies and the individuals who comprise them.

The one and indispensable way to correct the predicament of uncertainty is to get the objective clearly in mind, the duties unmistakeably assigned, the navigational charts out and understandable, the machinery in order, the power on and the message loud and clear for everyone to see and hear. Communication.

As Mr. Auger points out in this book, his extensive experience in the business world leads him to the distinct conclusion that there is a definite correlation between successful companies and those who have developed effective internal communications.

Well said, but how?

Our experience at 3M tells us that there is no more vital a management tool with which to turn on the navigational lights of effective communication than that of the properly planned and executed business meeting.

Meeting participants can be made clearly aware of company goals and the specific role and responsibilities of each in that endeavor. Valuable ideas can be exchanged. Problems pinpointed. Staff personnel can be trained, their abilities evaluated and potential future leaders discovered in this important forum.

In fact, every business executive has a responsibility to himself and his company to become a competent meeting leader for it is this ability which provides the very verve of a healthy and growing company and leads the way, resolutely, to established goals.

Business meetings have not acquired the most illustrious reputation. Not because there is anything inherently unsound in them, but because as with and other potential resource, satisfactory results are not likely to be obtained if that resource is not properly utilized.

Conducting a successful meeting need not be viewed with either apprehension or mystery. Sufficient experience permits a point-by-point guide in making every business meeting a rewarding and fruitful experience for all who participate in them.

This book is the result of serious study, testing and experimentation and is offered in the belief that it will considerably enhance the effectiveness of that most vital of all management tools — the business meeting.

Raymond H. Herzog
President
3M Company

CONTENTS

Chapter 1   **1** **Management in the Meeting Room**
             4   Meetings in the Stream of Work
             10 The Action Stream
             11 Summary

         2   **15** **Is This Meeting Necessary?**
             16 The Return on Investment
             21 When Not to Call a Meeting
             24 Meeting Participation
             26 Summary
             27 Conclusion

         3   **29** **Blueprinting the Successful Meeting**
             30 Developing the Strategy of the Meeting
             32 The Formal Agency
             36 Meeting Make-Ready
             38 Summary

         4   **41** **Where Minds Meet: The Conference Room**
             42 A Variety of Meeting Places
             49 Equipment for the Meeting Room
             52 Setting Up the Meeting

         5   **57** **The Skills of Leadership**
             59 Meeting Management
             61 Leadership Behavior
             65 Tips on Meeting Management
             71 Summary

         6   **73** **The Skills of Participation**
             74 Your Stake in Participation
             76 Prerequisite to Effective Participation
             77 Techniques of Active Participation
             80 Summary

7 **83** **Visual Aids to Clarity**
84 Some Principles of Visual Communication
87 Techniques that Emphasize the Man
94 Room Layout Guidlines

8 **101** **How to Make a Technical Presentation**
111 Summary

9 **115** **Communicating Financial Information**
117 What Management Needs to Know
122 Financial Reporting as an Organizational Product
124 Techniques of Data Presentation

10 **131** **Staff Meetings: Boon or Bore?**
132 Formula for Effective Staff Meetings
135 Aspects of Intimacy
136 Summary

11 **139** **Committee Meetings**
140 Committee Organization
143 Dynamic Maintenance of the Committee
144 Summary

12 **147** **The Sales Spectacular**
149 Multi-Media
152 Planning for a Sales Meeting
155 Execution of the Meeting
157 Sales Meeting Check List

13 **165** **Post-Meeting Follow-Through**
168 The Minutes of the Meeting
170 Follow-Ups After the Meeting
171 Summing Up.

Appendix **173** **The Art of a Good Visual**

Management in the Meeting Room

The late comedian Eddie Cantor once remarked, "some things you just can't change and pretending that you have is like painting stripes on a horse and calling it a Zebra."

Fundamentally, there are two kinds of change. One is the kind we set out to bring about. The other is the kind to which we have to adapt, willingly or otherwise.

Perhaps the most unchangeable but fundamental element in human relationships, whether it be in business, government, education, science or the arts, is the necessity of effective communications. It is by this process that we reach understanding, convert ideas into reality and plans into action.

A business acquaintance of mine recently told of an interview he had engaged in with an unusually curious reporter who was determined to discover who the real Mr. X was.

After some rather innocuous questions, at one point in the interview the reporter looked up from his notes and in rapid fire shot out the interrogatory, "Mr. X, what do you think is the worst thing in the world?"

Well, now, that is not a question most of us would want to answer without some reflection.

But I know what my answer would be if the question were to be answered in the context of the business world. I would unhesitatingly describe the worst affliction which can plague business as the lack of effective in-company communication.

From my experience in observing business operations throughout the country I cannot draw any other conclusion but that there is a definite relationship between those companies aglow with achievement and forward movement and those who have developed effective internal communications.

You can practically sense, the instant you walk through the door of an on-the-go company, the dynamic interplay and enthusiasm that pervades the atmosphere. It is obvious that the communications apparatus is on and signaling bright and clear.

Conversely, how sad to observe companies with good growth potential stagnating, or slipping farther and farther behind because they have sealed their members up in air-tight cubicles.

My next lament would be for the black eye which the business meeting, as such, has received over the years, not because its intrinsic value as an indispensable vehicle for communications does not still hold, unchangeable, but because the vehicle itself has not been properly utilized.

As with the horse with the painted stripes, no matter how badly the business meeting has been painted, it does not alter the fact that, properly planned and executed, it remains a vital management tool for effective communication.

In this respect, I am reminded of the philosopher's caveat "not to throw away the baby with the dirty bathwater."

Let's examine what the vehicle of the properly planned and executed business meeting can do toward developing good communication within your organization.

Some maintain it futile to plan because the future is unknown but they must be willing to accept all the surprises, anxieties and failures that accompany allegiance to that philosophy.

Some are content to trust in pure luck.

Take the case of the London cockney who was asked during World War Two if he weren't rather frightened that a Nazi bomb might drop on his home during one of the blitzes.

"Well, no Guvnor," he replied. "You see, I count me chances. Jerry has got to take off all right, ain't he? Then 'e's got to cross the Channel — and that ain't too easy for him. Then 'e's got to get by the coast. Then comes the Thames estuary, and that ain't all he likes. Then comes London. He can't miss that. But then 'e's got to find Ammersmith, then Acacia road, then number 87———and them most likely, I'll be at the pub."

But seriously, the case for planning and in some measure controlling the destiny of man has been made succinctly and well by some of the best minds of history.

Barrow wrote that "chance never wrote a legible book, never built a fair house, never drew a neat picture, never did any of these things, and never will."

William Penn held that "Dispatch is the life of business and method is the soul of dispatch. Method and dispatch govern the world," he maintained, and "Method goes far to prevent trouble in business for it makes the task easier, hinders confusion, saves abundance of time, and instructs those who have business depending, what to do — and what to hope."

Goethe echoed Penn when he said, "method will teach you to win time." Talleyrand said, "methods are masters of masters" and Mr. Simmons agreed, saying "method facilitates every kind of business — and by making it easy — makes it agreeable — and also successful."

Mr. G. K. Chesterton summed up his feelings about fate when he wrote, "I do not believe in a fate that falls on men however they act, but I do believe in a fate that falls on them unless they act."

We live in ever swiftening times. Developments which in the past required fifty years to bring about now may occur in six months. And this trend probably will continue.

In only the next few weeks countless patents will be granted, trademarks registered, new products announced, businesses incorporated, fail or disappear through merger. All businesses will be affected by these developments.

These conditions deem it imperative to utilize an orderly process for moving ahead. The business meeting can and should be an integral part of this process.

The process is this: Setting objectives and then working towards them. The concept revolves around two basic ideas: One is that the better you understand what it is you are trying to accomplish, the greater your chances of accomplishing it. The other is that progress can only be measured in terms of what one is trying to make progress toward.

There are three stages to generating an orderly communications process.

One: Individuals and their superiors at all levels determine and agree upon some specific results that are to be accomplished by some designated future date.

Two: The individuals set about to achieve these results with high hopes and great enthusiasm because in the course of program development, they have become thoroughly committed to it.

Three: At regular intervals results are measured against the objectives.

In this orderly process, the business meeting can be the vital vehicle in establishing, implementing and assessing achievement of goals. Further, it is the business meeting which permits clearly defining roles and responsibilities, exchange of ideas, pinpointing of problems, training of staff personnel, assessment of individual abilities and discovery of potential future leaders.

Meetings in The Stream of Work

When two people are engaged in a discussion, you would not ordinarily call that a meeting — even though your secretary might protect you from a caller by saying you are "in a meeting." The kinds of meetings we will discuss in this book are those which bring together a number of people with a definite communication purpose in mind. In fact, that's one of the first tests of a worthwhile meeting — whether it has a definite purpose.

There is value in defining meetings. When you do so you find they serve a variety of purposes, each calling for its own technique to yield the greatest return on investment. All meetings should bring about some change in the existing state of mind of the participants. Merely holding a meeting because it's "time" is not only wasteful but demoralizing to all concerned.

To illustrate how meeting goals and procedures depend upon the purpose of the meeting, let's examine the half-dozen basic kinds of meetings to be covered in separate chapters of this book. These are: *1. staff meetings, 2. information meetings, 3. fact-finding meetings, 4. problem-solving and decision-making meetings, 5. committee meetings, and 6. major sales meetings.*

Staff meetings, those captive assemblies in which the boss and his immediate crew are brought together for a weekly or monthly ordeal, are probably the most important type of business meeting. In some organizations these are chain-of-command meetings which begin at the first line of supervision and work their way up to the pinnacle. The staff meeting brings people together who have a common, continuing work relationship. It is an excellent tool for making a specific recommendation, for securing approval of a proposed project, and for communicating to another level of management. However, staff * meetings can be wasteful if participants are not given a chance to do some preparing in advance. An agenda published ahead of the meeting would remedy this by serving as a guideline for making the necessary preparations. Such meetings are also wasteful when topics are discussed that are not of concern to more than one staff member at a time, or when they are conducted merely because it is Monday morning or the first Friday of the month — whether or not there is really anything useful to discuss.

Information meetings are used by management to tell employees about important new decisions or about company activities of which they should be aware, or to persuade them to a course of behavior or attitude of mind desired by management. In essence, the aim is to put over a company point of view and have it accepted as their own by the employees. Such meetings can be effective when they succeed in getting the employees to identify their own interests with those of the company. On the other hand, these meetings are not likely to succeed when they are not well prepared, when they are poorly presented, or when they fail to show the listeners how their own best interests are at stake.

Fact-finding meetings are conducted when management wants to tap the experiences of several people at the same time to obtain facts for management planning and decision making. For example, if management calls in all of its sales representatives it wants to know about such vital matters as business conditions, competition, customer desires and complaints. If management were having trouble in a specific operation, it might call a conference of all the key people who have knowledge of that situation to get their reactions. Of course, such meeting purposes may come up on the agenda of a meeting called for an entirely different purpose, such as a sales meeting or a regular staff meeting. A fact-finding meeting is more likely to pay off when the participants are told what the problems are beforehand and are urged to come prepared.

Problem-solving and decision-making meetings call for the participation of people who are expected to contribute specialized points of view arising out of their separate experiences and responsibilities. Such meetings can be most effective when they are limited to the least number of people who represent a comprehensive grasp of the problem at hand. As with fact-finding meetings, these also are most likely to be productive when the participants have been given their assignments in sufficient time to enable them to do some homework before they come together. Unfortunately, too many meetings of this type are used by management personnel to pass the buck, avoiding a personal decision. In the final analysis, the task of decision making falls upon the shoulders of some individual who has organizational responsibility, since a conference itself cannot be held responsible. The purpose of the conference is to ascertain and review the facts, to identify the issues, and to discuss the probable gains and losses if alternative actions are taken. Oddly, unless such meetings are carefully managed, each participant may leave with a different understanding of what has been decided. Nevertheless, this category of meeting offers the greatest opportunity for the development of management skills; when the technical, sales, finance, and production experts are exposed to one another's problems, each carries away from the meeting a comprehensive picture of the business. But, again, this will occur only if the meeting is carefully managed. Individual viewpoints, and the meeting as a whole, should point to clear conclusions.

Committee meetings cover a wide range of activities but have certain pitfalls. Some are policy making, some are for audit and review, some to make decisions of award. Quite often they include representation from different departments. The most common pitfall of the committee system is that it tends to dilute the distribution of management responsibility. It is too easy to pass the buck to a committee in order to avoid or postpone difficult decisions. Committees are often criticized for continuing in existence long after their original purpose has been served. Some managements review their justification at regular intervals, while others do so whenever a senior executive begins to feel that "there are just too many committees around here." Even when a committee continues to justify its existence, there should be a constant infusion of new blood to enliven the committee and prevent it from falling into a rut. It might also be useful to have a recurring question on the agenda of every committee meeting: Should the committee continue to exist?

The *sales meeting* is the major event that brings together all of the marketing personnel on a regional or national basis to kick off a new product line or to unfold plans for the season or the year. Don't be afraid to mix selected technicians, production men, and other non-marketing personnel into these meetings. It exposes them to the total business picture. The major purpose of a sales meeting is to announce sales targets and stimulate the reaching of those targets. In part, the sales meeting is informational, in part promotional, and in part it is fact finding; bringing together all of the selling personnel enables management to canvass the total marketing situation. Locally sales managers may hold weekly or monthly sales meetings to keep track of activity. These meetings usually depend on more personal interrelationships and communication procedures. The larger sales spectaculars may run to great expense — thousands or tens of thousands of dollars and sometimes much more. They may sometimes take months of preparation, involving a great deal of planning and rehearsel. There is no second bite at the apple. A bad sales meeting can be a most demoralizing event. There's not much consolation in saying you'll do better next time.

The Fluid Pattern of Meetings

Actually, there is no rigid pattern of meetings in an organization. Sometimes a meeting takes on a mixed character with information, persuasion, fact finding, and decision making all wrapped up in the same agenda. The important thing is advance planning and preparation. All too often someone calls a meeting informally because of a spot crisis or because he needs help in framing a reply to an important letter. One or two people may be called in to put their shoulders to the wheel. If the vehicle doesn't budge more people may be called in until you wind up with a whole room full of people, including some who don't quite understand why they are there. What started out as a conversation between two may wind up as a full-fledged assembly of high-priced talent.

Another characteristic of a meeting is that it may be a single event in a very much larger stream of activity. For example, a meeting with field sales personnel may produce information that tells the management that it has a problem. This is then referred to a management conference which decides what to do about the problem. In turn, other meetings may be held with research and developement, production, and marketing personnel — depending on the magnitude of the original problem. Finally, meetings with the field sales personnel let them know what came out of all this effort and what they are now expected to do about it. Hence, it can be seen that meetings are not ends in themselves. Nor are they burdens to bear on top of other work loads. Rather, they are part of the ongoing stream of company activity. They are means through which the best thinking of the organization is brought together in order to move at least one step forward along the path to progress and profitable operation.

Every meeting must pay its own way. It should have a definite purpose clearly defined beforehand, so that the results of the meeting can be evaluated accurately. In fact, after a while you begin to anticipate the probable results of the meeting and if they do not look as if they will be worthwhile, you don't hold the meeting.

Meetings and Executive Development

As you read this book, if you keep in mind that a meeting is a serious undertaking that must make its contribution to the profit picture, you will perceive more clearly the situations in which meetings can serve as important training grounds and instill confidence in those men who have the potential to rise in the company. Opportunities for executive development will be found through participation in the planning of a meeting, the actual conduct of the meeting, and the follow-through which assures the payoff.

The Man's Point of View

It's interesting to watch people handle themselves in a meeting when they think their performance is being evaluated. This is acutely true in a sales meeting. Some men come in thinking that their performance may be under scrutiny. If they feel they haven't been doing well, this feeling may haunt them all through the meeting. (Or perhaps they may feel they've been doing well enough but management wants to put the squeeze on them to do better!) Their preparation for the meeting is to build up a strong defensive position. They may produce a good story, a series of alibis — why things aren't what they ought to be. They may get quite heated up about it if they have already succeeded in brainwashing themselves into believing their own alibis. This dealer is bad, that price is too high, quality is bad, the competition has something better at less cost, and so forth. The irony is that sometimes a man gets into this defensive frame of mind when he really has done fairly well.

Even though a sales meeting can be an important fact-finding source for management about conditions in the market, one man may use the meeting as a sound board for all his problems in the field. Even though he may be presenting useful information, you are never quite sure how useful it is when there is an element of defensiveness in his griping.

The man who shines brightly in the eyes of management at the same meeting will say, "This is my situation — these are my customers — here's what I've been doing — and here's the degree of success I've had."

But he won't stop there. He will display his creative potential by means of a constructive self-analysis. He will say what he thinks could be done in his market area and what he proposes to do about it. He may also suggest some constructive improvements management might take. Self-analysis coupled with what he has to say about management is more believable. He will not sound like a "gripe artist."

An important distinction between the two different types of men that have just been described is that one is somehow unable to think beyond his immediate situation, even though he may have the potential for doing much better. The other, by contrast, thinks and acts in terms of the broader company situation. When he gets up to talk, you recognize immediately that he has a complete picture that may include the company marketing program or an understanding of business conditions in his market area or some other incisive view. He is not afraid to depart, for the moment, from his own role as a salesman. He is talking *company* and he is effective in his presentation. Such a man is the kind that management taps for new posts.

The Alert Manager

Each supervisor and each manager above him is on the alert for men who stand out as "comers." Each company and each situation has its own motivations. In a growth situation, you're looking for men with ideas, men with the demonstrated capacity to tackle and solve new problems. You're looking for men who can give evidence of successfully directing other men. If you're aiming for sales growth, you're looking for sales supervisors, sales managers, marketing executives — men who can run some phase of the business rather than just remaining field salesmen.

As I travel around the country I meet with our field organization four times a year. At these meetings I have my only chance to engage in my own intra-company talent hunt. For me, these meetings cannot be just "information" meetings. I see my job as creating the *climate* which will enable these men to step out of their individual roles as salesmen — giving them the background which will enable them to speak in terms of a broader operating picture. When I meet with them I'm as interested in seeing them perform as in obtaining information. This is also true of meetings I attend in various departments of the home office and in plants away from our headquarters. The scarcity of talent requires the manager to be constantly on the alert for promising individuals. All potential sources of talent are important.

These meetings are just about the only opportunity a manager gets to evaluate his men when they are scattered around the country. In other management situations there are other opportunities to see men in action, as for instance when men are working together in the same office, exchanging memoranda, turning in reports, making recommendations, trouble shooting, etc. Out of all of this you make appraisals of the development of the man. Yet the meeting offers a unique opportunity to see the individual performing among his fellows — analyzing situations, presenting ideas, persuading others to points of view and to action.

The Action Stream

Listening is an important part of participating in a meeting, whether as man or manager. Recently I attended a meeting in Denver where we had all of our field men in for an ordinary sales meeting. Although we worked up an agenda, we never knew exactly what was going to come up in terms of currents of observation or comment. At this meeting, six of the field men gave status reports on their areas. In a sense, you could call this an information-gathering meeting — at this stage, anyway. All of these men had the same thing to say: our product line had two gaps in it. We needed a more deluxe line of these particular materials if we were going to best competition.

The indentification of this need was not on the agenda. It came out of alert discussion. We encouraged the men to talk, and as they sensed our interest, they pitched harder to us.

Later, somewhere between Denver and St. Paul, I got together with two other members of our organization, with whom I conducted a preliminary ''problem-solving'' meeting. We evaluated the idea that was generated at the Denver meeting and concluded this was something we'd better kick up the line.

Back at the home office we set up meetings with the people who could bring about the change that was recommended in Denver. We met with research and development people. They always want to know more about customer interests as reported by the field salesmen. They tell you some of their problems and you give them more information. Our of this discussion came a decision to commit laboratory effort to fill the gaps in the product line.

This is management in action. It takes place through a network of meetings, both formal and informal. Such meetings are not ends in themselves, but each yields its own creative fraction that forms the basis for additional discussion — always moving a step forward toward a final solution.

Summary

There is no element in the business world as necessary to realization of company objectives as effective in-company communications.

No venture, business or otherwise, is likely to succeed if those involved do not clearly understand what it is they are supposed to accomplish, and how.

It is the author's viewpoint, from years of observation, that there is a definite relationship between those companies who experience continuing success and growth and those who have developed effective in-company communications.

In a real sense, it is this element which turns on the company lights so that everyone in the endeavor can clearly see the goals and perceive his role and responsibility in the effort.

Lack of communication can only result in confusion and maladministration.

Good communication produces understanding, clears away confusion and uncertainty, permits ideas to be converted into reality and plans into action.

Similarly, it is the business meeting, properly planned and executed, which is the vital vehicle in realizing effective communication.

It is in this important forum that all of the elements necessary to a successful enterprise can be brought together to form a united company thrust.

Goals can be established, implemented and assessed. Roles and responsibilities can clearly be defined. Ideas can be exchanged, needs identified, and problems pinpointed. Staff personnel can be trained, abilities measured and potential future leaders discovered. Attitudes can be developed or altered.

Facts necessary for intelligent management planning and decision making can be obtained.

Despite past disparagement of the business meeting, it remains a fundamental communications tool. Business meetings need not be either a mystery or a chore. But they will be only as good or bad as they are permitted to be by those who plan and execute them.

This book is a communications effort to show the reader how business meetings can and will produce rewarding results by following the guidelines contained herein.

Notes

Notes

Chapter II

Is This Meeting Necessary?

It is very easy to say that every meeting should have a good reason — or not be held. The trick is pinpointing the good reason. Too many meetings are called because they become routine — it's that time of the week or month. Many are called in response to the pressing of a panic button.

A meeting requires the use of a valuable resource — the cost of the time of the attendees. It deserves at least the same careful consideration as the purchase of a new piece of equipment, another sort of investment. Each should yield a calculated return.

In this chapter, we take up three principal questions, each related to the others:

1. Why are you having the meeting? Unless you can identify a clear purpose — a net gain from the expenditure of time — don't call it.

2. When should you not call a meeting, even though it seems to serve a useful purpose? Are all the conditions and circumstances right? Is there a better way:

3. Who should participate in a particular meeting? Are you planning to have the right participants?

The Return on Investment

Have I a good reason for a meeting? This is only one of the screening questions you should ask yourself before you decide to call a meeting. Nevertheless, this is an important starting point, for it enables you to prepare well, it gives you a criterion for monitoring the costs of the meeting, and it provides a standard for evaluating accomplishments. Most of the legitimate reasons for calling a meeting can be found in the following checklist:

1. To receive reports from participants.
2. To reach a group judgment as the basis for a decision.
3. To discover, analyze or solve a problem.
4. To gain acceptability for an idea, program or decision.
5. To achieve a training objective.
6. To reconcile conflicting views.
7. To provide essential information for work guidance, or for the relief of insecurities or tensions.
8. To assure equal understanding by all present.
9. To obtain immediate reactions when speedy response to a problem is important.
10. To have an excuse for taking up a matter which has gotten stalled.
11. To advance the course of management, i.e., to run the business.

To Receive Reports

Since you can obtain information by mail, inter-office correspondence, and telephone, you should have a more constructive reason for bringing people together than merely to receive information. The most important reason would be that you would expect each report by a participant to stimulate both thinking and discussion by other participants. A report-type meeting should lead to a common understanding of mutual problems for the benefit of the participants as well as for the meeting leader who represents management.

An oral presentation may enable participants to convey more information than they could through written memoranda. The participants can bring in exhibits. An oral presentation can often be given more effectively and memorably. Some men can be more expressive when they can point to a chart or use an overhead projector.

While it is entirely appropriate to have a man-to-man report without pulling a lot of other people into a meeting, there is something about the psychology of a group presentation that impels the meeting participant to be more thoughtful in his preparation. Knowing this, the astute meeting leader can use the excuse of an open forum as a means of finessing a stalled individual into bringing some matter to a head. The meeting leader can also use reports to provoke certain desired reactions on the part of the listeners.

To Reach a Group Judgment

In a sense, every meeting should lead to a decision. This can be a decision on a particular problem given to the group, or it can be a personal decision on the part of each participant concerning his future attitudes or his future course of action. We are concerned here, however, with group participation in decision making. The advantage of a meeting is that it gives everyone who has a critical stake in the decision an opportunity to express himself. Either you get a variety of input to help decide the matter, or you get simultaneous reactions to a decision which has tentatively been formulated.

To Discover, Analyze, or Solve a Problem

The problem-solving meeting may start out with a clearly identified problem in need of a solution or it may begin at the opposite extreme examining the symptoms of a condition that needs clarification. The group performs a useful function in bringing together the bits and pieces of experience and insight which may lead to common understanding. One person may describe an effect, while another suggests a plausible reason for it. Out of a pattern of this type of analysis, an acceptable cause-and-effect relationship may be discovered. On the other hand, a participant might bring in parallel experiences which suggest an entirely different analysis. In this type of meeting, the important thing is to get a well-balanced interplay of ideas, experiences, supporting facts, contradictions and insights.

To Gain Acceptability

It is well known that when people have to carry out a decision, the manner in which they do so is governed by their attitudes. Opposition to a decision, for any reason, may be expressed through grudging compliance or through outright sabotage, depending on how much a man feels that his personal security or self-esteem is at stake. On the other hand, agreement with a decision is normally given effect through forms of action ranging from willing compliance to unbridled enthusiasm.

It is an axiom of management that you are most likely to obtain the best compliance upon the part of those who are going to have to carry out a decision if they have contributed in some way to making the decision. It is not necessarily important that all agree with the decision. It is more important that each should have had a chance to be heard — to get an oar in. Of course, if the final decision is to a participant's own liking, so much the better, Even though you have reached a tentative decision, you may still find it important to call a discussion meeting, if only to enhance the conditions of acceptability.

Once you've called the meeting, however, you must make it clear that the matter is genuinely open for discussion. You must be prepared to reverse or modify your decision if the discussion brings out ample justification for this. No man's opinions, including your own, are sacred.

To Achieve a Training Objective

In some measure every meeting has a training value for all who participate. In fact, many managers utilize the meeting specifically for personnel development. Sometimes they call a meeting because they want to force their people to cope with difficult problems. This will occur most frequently when kicking off a new program, or when dry-running the applications of new policies and procedures.

The meeting is also a means through which new staff members can be exposed to group reactions. Men who are being groomed for higher responsibility can be given an opportunity, without additional expenditure of effort, to observe how their seniors engage in decision making.

Not to be overlooked is the valuable teaching tool inherent in the meeting. The teaching role of management is a continuous proposition, the purpose of which is to provide instruction which will make others more valuable to themselves and to those for whom they work.

Organization of thought, definition of goals is at the root of effective communication and any successful meeting presupposes organization of materials to be presented and goals defined.

It is at the meeting, then, where management can exercise its teaching role to instruct others to organize their thoughts and materials and in so doing become effective communicators.

The use of visual aids also can be of great assistance in organization of materials, conservation of time and more effective communication.

Visual aids promote organization because:

1. They force order and sequence in the presentation.

2. They require selection and itemization of key ideas while guarding against the omission of other vital points.

3. They conserve time by keeping the speaker on the track and to the point.

4. Last, but not least, they instill confidence in the speaker, lessen self confusion and promote the habit of essential thinking.

To Reconcile Conflicts

In business life the meeting room replaces the dueling field. When there is a sharp difference of views, the principal contenders can be brought together for constructive discussion. The opponents may themselves want a way out, in which case some of the other participants may be counted upon to offer face-saving proposals. Even when the contenders are expected to maintain opposing views, balanced group discussion brings in other viewpoints and — in the hands of a skilled leader — provides opportunities for relieving tension. If the latter is the only accomplishment of the meeting, it may be regarded as a successful one.

To Provide Information

Since so much information is transmitted through words on paper, the meeting that transmits information has a special virtue. The personality of the communicator can be the decisive element — a little inspiration mixed in with a great deal of information. The informational-type meeting might be desirable to obtain immediate reactions to an announcement; the seriousness of a situation can be underscored by a well-timed presentation. More effective communication can often be achieved through the use of visual displays and projections rather than through "hard copy" reproduction in a printed document.

To Assure Equal Understanding

The informational meeting does help assure that all of the participants are given the same opportunity for understanding. When groups are small enough, however, understanding can be enforced by encouraging open discussion, especially through questions and answers. Such give-and-take can help avoid the confusion which often arises when people understand the same words differently. Sometimes we try to understand things as we want to understand them. Sometimes we attach meanings which were never intended. Semantics, unfortunately, remains an inexact science, but the risks of misunderstanding can be held to a minimum in a meeting which encourages open discussion.

To Obtain Quick Reactions

When the panic button is pressed — and what organization does not have a supply of them? — the first impulse often is, call a meeting! This is in order when participation of a number of people is needed with least delay. There are many situations when a quick group response is needed to a proposed action. Of course there are many, many situations in which the matter is not really one of panic-button urgency, but one in which time must be telescoped. A decision has been reached, for example, but before it is put into effect, a ratification is desired; or a last quick check is sought to button up a decision.

To Break Administrative Log Jam

This one must be used sparingly. If you frequently have to resort to meetings in order to get around people who could make decisions on their own, you probably have a case for administrative reorganization. If someone should be making decisions without benefit of meetings and is not doing so, the meetings become a subterfuge and everybody knows it. Nevertheless, the business of the organization must go on, even when nothing is done about people who do not exercise responsibility. The meeting then becomes a convenient medium through which to bring up a matter which otherwise will remain "pending."

As a variation of this theme, you may have people who ordinarily are excellent decision makers, but who are unable to move on specific items. Perhaps they are personally affected, or perhaps they are being forced to make unpopular decisions. In such cases, without making a habit of it, the people in the organization will sense and accept the legitimacy of passing a matter to a meeting instead of putting that person on the spot.

It is conceivable, of course, that all or many of the foregoing might be the reasons for calling a particular meeting. It is just as possible that only one of the foregoing might justify the meeting, but the greatest likelihood is that there will be two or more reasons for calling any meeting.

When Not to Call a Meeting

The bird of time has but a little way
To flutter – and the bird is on the wing.

From Omar Khayyam comes this delightful verse — the same poet who gave us the more heady lines about a book of verse, a loaf of bread, a jug of wine and thou. . .

In many thousands of offices throughout the country, one can see a sign with the simple work THINK, courtesy of the International Business Machines Corporation. It might be a good idea if one could make a little sign for the tens of thousands of conference rooms which would read THE BIRD IS ON THE WING.

Think About the Cost

Have you ever thought about the actual costs of a meeting that accomplishes little or nothing? If you have six people in a meeting whose average salary is $10,000, the cost of the conference in terms of base pay alone for one hour is $28.80. This, however, is only part of the story. To the base figure you must add payroll taxes, fringe benefits, and general overhead. Some part of the time of the man's secretary should be included, as well as the time he spends going to and from the meeting, in addition to preparing for it. As a rule of thumb, to get the cost of a meeting you should double the value of the pay.

Cost of a Meeting to Nearest Dollar, per Hour								
Average Pay	Number of Participants							
	10	9	8	7	6	5	4	3
15,000	144	130	115	101	86	72	58	43
12,500	120	108	96	84	72	60	48	36
10,000	96	86	77	67	58	48	38	28
7,500	72	65	58	50	43	36	29	22

The accompanying table can be used as a ready computer of the cost of a meeting. To it should be added any special preparatory costs. There is no way of telling, however, just how much is lost in productive activity to which attention was not given. These are cold, sobering figures. Multiply by the numerous meetings which these executives must attend to see the true significance of these figures. They should make us pause to make sure that there is not some alternative to holding a meeting — an alternative which would be just as effective, considering the cost.

Alternates to Meetings

Four alternatives to calling a meeting are these:

1. Personal executive action.
2. Written communication.
3. Individual telephone calls.
4. Conference telephone calls.

Personal executive action should be standard procedure for run-of-the-mill decision-making matters. Meetings should be reserved for new policy and procedure and for matters whose complexity, uncertainty, or importance call for the participation of a number of people. The meeting definitely should not be used as a means for passing the buck. When executive action is in order, it has the additional advantage of being faster.

Written communications can be used for sending information up or down the line of command. Among memos' advantages are uniformity, authoritativeness, and permanence. They minimize the risk that subtleties of communication may be lost when people make their own notes — or fail to — after participation in a meeting. They overcome the tendency for communications to become distorted when they are passed on by word of mouth after a meeting. They can be written at the convenience of their authors and read at the convenience of their recipients; it is not necessary to assemble all of the recipients at some risk of interrupting essential work. Finally, they add to the written record of the development of a company's business affairs.

Of course, written communications also have disadvantages. Words on paper that carry clear meanings for the originator may convey entirely different meanings to readers. As compared to meetings, there is little opportunity for clarifying the communication through easy give-and-take. Then, too, many people find it so difficult to express themselves on paper that they omit useful information that would have been readily presented in a spoken form.

For spot communication, the telephone is the indispensable medium of business relationships. The caller and receiver can raise and answer questions without having to leave their desks. Except for the brief moments of discussion, the business of the organization keeps on with minimum interruption. Even for long distance calls, telephone communication can be much cheaper than writing letters and infinitely cheaper than travel. You might well consider a conference telephone call as an economical alternative to the costs of bringing a number of people in from different cities for a meeting at headquarters. When video communication becomes more common, the conference call meeting is likely to become more popular. Still, nothing really takes the place of the human interaction of people in each other's physical presence.

Readiness Factors

Good preparation for a meeting may be nine-tenths of the success formula. The next chapter will be devoted entirely to this important aspect of meetings. It is one of the things to consider when you plan the timing of a meeting. If you are not ready for it — if you are not going to have matters in order so that the best advantage is derived from the time to be spent, the meeting should either be deferred or not held at all.

Will all of the key participants be available? Will someone be unavailable whose contribution is so important that the meeting should not be held? Are you allowing enough time for the participants to prepare themselves for the meeting? Will special materials or facilities that are needed be ready? Is the timing strategic? Are there things which should be done or announced before the meeting is held? Conversely, should the meeting be held before certain other events transpire?

Strategy Factors

Innumerable other factors can argue for or against calling a meeting at all or at any given time. The executive lives in a world of dynamic interplay. He is concerned with the impression he creates and with timely impact. As already mentioned, he may not want to have a meeting unless certain key personalities are present, but there may also be occasions when it is important not to have a meeting when certain people *are* present. Each situation is a law unto itself. The executive must relate the meeting and its impact to the larger strategy of his working plans and activities, recognizing that these must be in the best interests of his company.

Occasionally there are situations in which expediency governs. Thinking through what may come up in a meeting, you may decide that a clash of personalities is inevitable and that this clash should be avoided. Short of a clash, someone may be deeply embarrassed. You might consider it better to have a private conference with the individual affected, or you might decide that the interests of the organization take precedence. Fortunately, such considerations do not apply to most meetings.

Meeting Participation

For most meetings you can make up a routine attendance list based upon people's assignments and functional interests. The subject matter of the meeting governs. For effectiveness, however, you may need to increase or decrease the number of participants.

General Criteria for Participation

From the standpoint of good communication, keep in mind that the more people you add, the more difficult it becomes for them to talk to one another. The growth of complexity is vastly disproportionate to the number of people added. Would you believe that adding only one or two people might double or triple the burdens and complexities of communication? Over 30 years ago, a French management consultant named V. A. Graicunas worked out the mathematics of interrelationships in a group. He said: "Just why an executive already having four subordinates should hesitate before adding a fifth member to the group which he controls directly, becomes clear if it is realized that the addition not only brings twenty new relationships with him, but adds nine more relationships to each of his colleagues. The total is raised from 44 to 100 possible relationships for the unit, an increase in complexity of 127 percent in return for a 20 percent increase in working capacity."

These figures are applicable to problem-solving meetings and any others in which there is a cross-fire of discussion among the participants. In general, the more complex the subject matter or the more intimate the discussion, the fewer should be the participants. Conversely, the lower the amount of individual participation, the greater the number of people you can have at a meeting. Thus, if a meeting is scheduled merely to hear one speaker, you can have as many in the audience as the room will accommodate. However, as soon as you begin to look for audience participation, you have to start cutting back again.

Here are five criteria for participation in a meeting, any of which may be regarded as qualifying:

1. *The individual or his department is expected to carry out or take part in a decision to be reached at the meeting.*

2. *The individual possesses unique contributory information.* He may have had experience in similar situations, he may be familiar with certain conditions or operations, or he may know people or personalities whose responses need to be anticipated.

3. *His approval may be needed at the meeting*, or he may be someone whose subsequent approval will be required. He may be in the administrative line of command, or he may be someone whose professional or legal acquiescence will be needed.

4. *He has official responsibility for the matter under discussion.* That is, he is the one who ordinarily is paid to worry about the matter to be discussed.

5. *He has a personal contribution to make from a strategic standpoint.* He may be a knowledgeable idea man. He may be an elder statesman who can lend a certain stability to a meeting. He may be needed to balance off a controversial discussion or to provoke discussion.

Ordinarily, you need only one person to represent a particular point of view or subject-matter interest. Occasionally, you will see executives and others who come to meetings attended by personal entourages including knowledge-carriers and advisers. If they are absolutely required, they should not be seated directly at the meeting table, to cut down on the seeming participation.

Special Aspects of Participation

Should the boss and his subordinates participate in the same meeting as equals around the table? It is a moot question as to whether the subordinate can act as an equal under such conditions. He cannot help being mindful of the reactions of his immediate boss to anything he might say. So far as other participants are concerned, they would expect him to be a representative and adjunct of his immediate boss. The subordinate should never throw his boss off balance in a meeting. The general tendency is for meetings to be composed of people who have approximately equal status. A man brings his subordinate only when there is a special reason for so doing: to contribute first-hand knowledge, to be a technical adjunct, or to participate for special training purposes.

On controversial matters, there is an unwritten law that opposing points of view must be invited. There also are apt to be some people who have established special interests in the area of the controversy, so that omitting them would be regarded as an affront.

Summary

When to Call a Meeting

1. To define organization goals.
2. To receive reports from participants.
3. To reach a group judgment as the basis for a decision.
4. To discover, analyze or solve a problem.
5. To gain acceptability for an idea, program or decision.
6. To achieve a training objective.
7. To teach personnel to organize their thoughts and materials and clearly define goals in their meeting persentations.
8. To reconcile conflicting views.
9. To provide essential information for work guidance, or for the relief of insecurities or tensions.
10. To assure equal understanding of company policy, methods or decisions.
11. To obtain immediate reactions when speedy response to a problem is important.
12. To have an excuse for taking up a matter which has gotten stalled.
13. To advance the course of management, i.e., to run the business.

When Not to Call a Meeting

1. When other communications, such as telephone, telegram, letter, memo, etc., will produce the desired results.
2. When there is not sufficient time for adequate preparation by participants or meeting leader.
3. When one or more key participants are not available.
4. When timing is not right.
5. When the meeting is not likely to produce satisfactory results in view of clashing personalities or larger management strategy.
6. When, in view of cost of meeting, net return is not likely to be realized.

1. An individual or his department who is expected to carry out a decision to be reached at the meeting.

2. One who possesses unique contributory information.

3. One whose approval may be needed at the meeting.

4. One who has an official responsibility for the matter under discussion.

5. One who has a personal contribution to make from a strategic standpoint.

Conclusion

In brief, you call a meeting when there is a specific, definable management purpose to be served in so doing. In some way you expect the meeting achievements to warrant the time and expense of participation. A business meeting should be a *tool* of management but *never* a replacement for it.

Timing is of the essence. Conditions must be just right, involving people and the situation as a whole. Just as the meeting must pay its way, so must each participant contribute to the success of the meeting. Remember, one of your continuing responsibilities as a manager is the development of future managers. For this, the meeting room can be your most important training ground.

Notes

Chapter III

Blueprinting the Successful Meeting

In 1785, Robert Burns wrote a delightful poem. "To a Mouse," in which he said:

> *The best laid schemes o'mice and men*
> *Gang aft a-gley:*
> *An'lea'e us nought but grief and pain,*
> *for promis'd joy.*

The moral to be drawn is that the way to minimize the frustration of hope is through careful planning based on a well-studied anticipation of what may transpire.

Much of your blueprinting at least a fairly clear concept of what you want to accomplish — will have been laid out for you once you have decided that the meeting has a logical purpose. In the preceding chapter, we provided a basis for judging the value of a proposed meeting and for determining in advance the probable contributions of participants. Here we will take up the actual planning of the meeting in detail. Your meeting is least likely to go "a-gley" if both planning and preparation are adequate. The three topics to be covered are: developing the strategy of the meeting, preparing the agenda, and readying both materials and participants.

Developing the Strategy of the Meeting

For purposes of illustration, we'll assume that we have an important meeting to engineer. The principles and techniques we'll cover are just as applicable to smaller meetings and even for those called "on the run," although obviously one can't do much advance planning for the impromptu meeting. However, the man who learns how to prepare well for the pre-arranged meeting will have developed an approach and a set of skills enabling him to cope with the unexpected. Much of what follows bears on the analysis of people — their motives and behavior. At first glance this might seem an elaborate analysis to make every time you want a meeting. Actually, once you get in the habit of thinking along these lines, you'll find yourself automatically building on a base of acquired knowledge and insight.

We need to make one additional assumption. This is that you are planning a meeting among people of approximately the same operating level, or that you are to have a meeting with your own staff. In either case, as planner, you are the one responsible for developing the strategy. If you are to participate in a meeting called by someone else, the analysis may help you achieve your own goals.

Goal Analysis

It is only too easy to assume that because a man is on the company payroll he is devoting himself entirely to the achievement of official goals and aims. We can hope so. But reality tells us that men are always trying to reconcile their personal goals with their official responsibilities. Ideally, the two serve each other. However, the ideal may remain out of reach because of the difficulty we all have in being completely objective not interpreting our treatment of company business to suit our private interests. Every meeting participant should realize that he is there to help the group get something accomplished. He should be prepared to contribute something to, and derive something from, the meeting.

The starting point for goal analysis is a definition of what you want to accomplish through a meeting. This you will have largely determined when you decided that the meeting was necessary. The next step is to assess the foreseeable barriers to accomplishment. Much of your planning will be devoted to overcoming these.

Suppose you are to call a problem-solving or a decision-making meeting. Who are the people affected by the proposed solution? What is each to gain and what might each lose? How important is each gain and each loss? How strongly might each participant fight to achieve one and prevent the other? Your clues to the most sensitive points may be found in the areas of probable change or adjustment. Who is being asked to change his methods? Who will be asked to forfeit something?

Narrowing down the issues, what are the critical points on which a decision might hinge? What must be traded off in order to obtain acceptance? Acceptance can be tangible and material or it can be symbolic — a matter of status or recognition; it can be a hope for a better future.

For additional clue-seeking, look to both successes and failures of the past. Bear in mind, though, that what worked in some other company, in some other department, or even in your own recent experience, might not work in the present situation. At least, not in all of its details. Each situation calls for an individual solution based on a careful review of current conditions in the total situation. While you look to past experience, ask yourself how the present situation differs.

The next step in analyzing the problems of goal achievement is to make a preliminary estimate of other hurdle factors. Under the best circumstances, given the present people and their resources, what are you likely to accomplish? Under what disadvantages will you be working? What else do you need? What must be done to make up for your inadequacies? Are your aspirations unrealistic?

Participant Analysis

Let's start by assuming that you are calling a meeting which will be attended by representatives of different departments. While all members of the same department do not think and express themselves identically, the chances are you'll get just about the same opinions from one representative as from another. Over a period of time, the group brainwashes itself. Through association and mutual guidance, the members of a group tend to acquire a common point of view. Hence, you can begin to predict how a man is likely to express himself if he comes from the accounting department, the personnel department, the sales department, the research department, or the production department. You can predict one response from a man who operates out of headquarters, while someone who works out of a branch office may be expected to have a different point of view. You can anticipate the positions to be taken by a man if you have a working knowledge of how his department has represented itself over the past, and how he personally plays the role a representative of his function and his own self interest. Of course, this is not ironclad; individual personalities differ.

A new man is like a body of water in which you must take soundings in order to learn how to navigate. He must be observed and appreciated in a variety of situations. Eventually he becomes predictable. You learn how to anticipate his reactions to given situations or challenges.

You can never expect to predict individual behavior with absolute certainty. If you do, you are in for painful surprises. Nevertheless, the business of a leader is to study men. Each situation is a laboratory in which a man reveals himself. Bit by bit, the structure of his own personality is uncovered. You must make a point of observing his behavior in each situation. Then when you are confronted by a particular problem sou will be able to take guidance from his previous responses and attitudes.

The analysis of each participant can be divided into three categories of information: 1. the position he is likely to take to represent his element of organization; 2. his personal goals and aspirations, and 3. his performance as a working personality.

Will he be on time, well prepared? Will he carry his load? Will he crowd the discussion? Is he easily provoked? Does he need to be pressed into expressing himself? Will it be necessary to have someone primed to balance off his point of view?

The Formal Agenda

By now the plot of your meeting should have been pretty well worked out. The agenda becomes a formality of planning — or does it? In practice, your agenda shapes up as you interact with the people from whom you must be getting the ideas for the meeting. From the very moment you begin to talk about the meeting or even to conjecture about it, you must have at least a mental outline of it.

The finished chairman's outline may be the basis of a more formal agenda to be circulated among participants when a number of topics are to be taken up.

Ostensibly, the agenda tells people what is to be taken up in the meeting. It also serves to control the time allotted to topics in a meeting which has a set time limit. These are the formal usages. Another, more important value of an agenda is that it serves to sound out reactions to discussion topics, particularly when they may be controversial. Sometimes you do not anticipate elements of controversy until you've had a reaction to the very idea of introducing them. If you would rather avoid controversy on a particular subject — at least for the moment — agenda planning gives you an excuse for orderly retreat.

From an engineering standpoint, the agenda serves as a medium for organizing speakers, topics, audience participation, visual aids, auxiliary equipment, and any special events within an allotted period of time.

Who Plans the Agenda

If you're to hold a regular staff meeting, do you have your secretary call the attendees to ask if they have anything for the meeting agenda? If so, did you ever think that this might be a confession that you do not know your own employees' problems? If you have a proper supervisory relationship, you will already know their working problems. From your knowledge of your own department, you are the chief planner. This doesn't mean that you do not invite suggestions for the meeting. Rather, you maintain something of an open-door relationship in which you make it easy for people to propose topics on their own initiative.

In preparation for our monthly division operating committee meeting, I personally like to publish an agenda with enough topics assigned to individuals to justify the meeting. I then ask for additional subjects that members might feel should also be considered at the meeting.

You should bear in mind that your department is a unity for which you are responsible. You are the one who develops and carries off its grand strategies and its minor strategies. You are also the one to be held accountable by your own superiors. While the participants should be made to feel that they have had an important hand in shaping the business of the department, this is really a matter of supervisory technique. You are almost in the position of the card-trick expert who makes you think that you are picking the cards which he is actually "forcing" upon you. The difference is that you really do want to sense reactions and to accommodate them whenever practicable.

It is extremely important that the preliminary groundwork and plans be well thought out before the meeting. In fact, a general rule of thumb suggests that the more important the meeting, the more necessary it is that this preliminary groundwork be accomplished.

However, a caution. One must not create the impression among the participants that the meeting has been so finally and rigidly preplanned that they are merely assembling to hear a proclamation. A delicate balance must be struck between thorough preplanning while leaving the impression among those attending that there is a legitimate need for the meeting and that their views, information and problem-solving talents can be considered. Again, a matter of supervisory technique.

When you are developing an agenda for a meeting to be attended by people who are not subject to your own administrative control, your problem may be different, although not necessarily so. As the meeting leader, you still have responsibility for its success. However, lack of direct control over all participants makes it necessary that you accede somewhat more to their various representative interests.

When you finally have the agenda worked out, it may have an assortment of side notes which identify for you points to be emphasized, points to play down, people to bring in a critical moments, important examples, and other essential information. Finally, you will have worked out a tentative time scale for the management of the meeting. This will be discussed below.

The Multiple Topic Agenda

The number of separate topics taken up in a meeting will be determined by their nature as well as by the purpose of the meeting itself. Suppose you arrange what we shall call a review meeting. A long list of items might be taken up, such as requests for the purchase of equipment, or the review of the sales performance of each participant. You might call a meeting which acts on claims or recommendations for awards. In such meetings, you allow enough time to cover the expected load, while you also tailor the load to the amount of time available. In any event, you might be taking up many small items. Regular staff meetings tend to take up a collection of business topics which have accumulated since the last meeting. They may also be designed to take up a single topic that is of interest to the entire group.

When you are to have an agenda containing a number of topics, it is someimes advisable to try to keep them all within the same area of subject matter. For one thing, this keeps meeting participation to a minimum. For another, it enables you to move smoothly from one related topic to another.

If the topics are unrelated, it is better to have fewer on your schedule. It is sometimes hard to switch the minds of participants from one topic to an entirely different one. You are less likely to get good preparation when you have a number of totally different topics. There is, besides, some limit to the absorption of important new ideas. Therefore, if possible, consider limiting discussion to perhaps one major item, with smaller items added which do not require extensive preparation in advance.

If a matter is of sufficient importance, it should be allowed to stand alone without undue competition. This is not always possible. For example, when you bring men in from all over the country, you try to take up as many important items of business as possible. Such meetings usually call for a long lead time for advance preparation. Because of the congestion of business, as with annual sales meetings, it may even be necessary to bring in some forms of light relief or semi-entertainment, including guest speakers, motion picture films, special exhibits and displays, etc.

Idea Files

From time to time matters come to our attention which, though suitable for discussion in a meeting, do not in themselves justify calling one.

A good way to handle these is to build up an idea file of clippings, reports on which you have encircled troublesome items, memoranda, performance analyses, problem papers, etc. These can be used to buttress your development of topics to which they are related, or they can be used as independent sources of ideas to be brought up as agenda topics in themselves. You will find this a convenient time-saver which you might well commend to your subordinates. It encourages them not only to think ahead to their participation in future meetings, but also to think about their work operations rather broadly.

How Long a Meeting

Meetings run from quickies a few minutes long to meetings that last several days. The chances are that the quickie-meeting will call for a minimum of planning and preparation, at least on the part of the people who attend. The longer the meeting, the more elaborate the preparation, so that in a sense, you should balance one off against the other.

On the whole, a compromise of all factors adds up to a meeting which should typically last about one hour. This is brief enough to hold the span of attention before people need to break for coffee or fresh air. A meeting that lasts an hour and a half may be already bordering on the edge of diminishing returns.

If you're allotting time to individual items on an agenda, plan to allow a longer period when the topics are highly controversial or highly complex. Anything utterly new may also call for longer discussion periods.

Meeting Make-Ready

The making of an agenda merely sets down on paper what you plan to accomplish in a meeting. Without an agenda, the most skilled meeting leader might not be able to bring off a meeting successfully. With an agenda, however, he is able to devote his talents to managing the interplay of personalities in the meeting room. He can do this more effectively because he knows what he wants to achieve. With this general strategy mapped out in the agenda, he can concentrate on the more fluid tactics of the meeting room.

For the regular meeting, no additional preparation is needed. For important meetings, however, the completion of an agenda may be only the preface to a great deal of careful groundwork before the actual meeting. If it is to be an important event, you can take nothing for granted. At the very least, you must be assured as to the preparation of participants, special speakers, special exhibits, and any unique "props" or materials which will be needed. Apart from this physical aspect, you may need to keep in touch with key participants in order to sense their thinking on key issues. This is particularly true where the participants are your own colleagues, over whom you do not exercise direct control.

Participant Briefing and Monitoring

Ordinarily the agenda should be communicated to the participants in advance of the meeting, but not too far in advance. For the simple meeting, it may be sufficient to inform participants that a single topic is to be discussed. For the more elaborate meeting, or to notify participants, a written arenda should be distributed about a week ahead of time. If extensive preparation, particularly of analyses and written materials, is required, more time will be needed, perhaps as much as a month. In some organizations, particularly as regards committee and board meetings, an agenda must be distrubuted together with attachments supporting each topic on the agenda. No item can then be brought up for discussion that the committee members have not been briefed on through this advance distribution.

How much follow-up is needed between distribution of the agenda and the actual meeting? This will depend upon your experience with individual participants. Some of them may regard this as an affront. Others need to be reminded or prompted, through subtle or direct means. On sensitive issues, where you want to anticipate problems that will arise in the meeting, you may want to find excuses to talk with participants in order to discover any particular problems they will bring up or controversial positions they will take.

There is a different type of situation in which you may want to hold rehearsals; for example, when you are going to make an important presentation personally or on a group basis. It is a good idea to use a stopwatch to time yourself and a tape recorder to enable you to play back your own presentation.

Special Arrangements

You should have a subsidiary agenda for your own pre-meeting guidance in which you list all of the items that need to be made ready. It might include outside speakers, special meeting facilities, preparation of visual aids, speech writing, rehearsals, arranging for films, procuring projection equipment, etc.

If you have a long list, it may be necessary to delegate follow-up responsibilities to one or more people besides yourself. In so doing, make sure no details are neglected because the areas of responsibility were not clearly defined.

Finally, here are some courtesy reminders which help maintain good relationships and also contribute to the probability of more successful meetings:

1. Avoid surprise meetings. They unhinge people from their regular work schedules. When meetings must be called on short notice, try to allow at least a day for participants to get ready, preferably two days. When you have to call real emergency meetings on a "drop everything" basis, they'll be taken more seriously if you are known to push the panic button sparingly.

2. Make sure participants are fully informed as to the purpose and subject matter of the meeting, whether by word of mouth or by written communication. Even if they do no more than think about the matter, they will at least have that amount of preparation.

3. If individual participants are to be called upon for statements

or presentations, tell them so individually beforehand. If possible, allow them some measure of choice or latitude.

4. Tell them just how long the meeting is to last, and then be sure to live within the estimate of time. If the meeting is out on time, the participants know you mean business.

Summary

In brief, these points should be kept in mind when blueprinting the meeting:

1. It should be carefully planned with a clear concept of what it is you want to accomplish.

2. The goals of both the company and the individual should be realized. The participant should contribute something to, and derive something from, the meeting.

3. Hurdles and barriers should be anticipated in advance and likely participant responses calculated from past experience.

4. Agenda should be organized well but not leave the impression that it is so cut and dried it precludes attendee participation. Agenda should be distributed in advance leaving ample preparation time.

5. In a multiple topic agenda allow time to cover topics and tailor load to amount of time available. Try to keep topics related. If unrelated, schedule fewer of them.

6. Subsidiary agenda should be made as a guideline when special arrangements, facilities or meeting aids are required.

7. Avoid surprise meetings. Participants should be notified in advance of the purpose, subject matter, their role in the meeting and how long it will last.

Notes

Notes

Chapter IV

Where Minds Meet: The Conference Room

The all-purpose ideal meeting room doesn't exist. If it can accommodate 500 people, it won't be good for 8 or 10. If it is an elaborate chart room in which the board of directors holds its meetings, it isn't the place for a department manager to have a meeting with his staff in order to review performance for the last quarter. If you build a meeting room into the floor plans of a new structure, it is likely to turn out later to be in the wrong place, or too small, or lacking the right outlets for electrical equipment. It turns out to be someone's wrong guess as to the different needs to be satisfied for different sizes of audiences and different types of visual displays.

You might provide a number of rooms, both large and small, to accommodate these statistical accidents of demand; yet you are sure to be frustrated because during one particular week just about the large conference rooms.

The moral of the story is that usually you have to make the best use of the available facilities. In fact, chances are most meetings are held in an office, routinely occupied by an executive, his desk, a work table, chairs, and a bookcase.

Whether a meeting is to be held in an elaborate room or an office, there are certain conditions and procedures that will contribute to its success or failure.

A Variety of Meeting Places

Conference rooms tend to be glamorized when discussed in books and articles on good management. One must wonder whether the writers themselves were ever subjected to the vicissitudes of everyday life in an office. Most ordinary conferences and meetings are held in conditions that are far from glamorous or ideal. Usually you make the best of what's available. Keep this in mind, therefore, as we go over some of the more ideal arrangements pertaining to meeting rooms. We will wind up with a practical discussion of the problems of adapting the typical office.

Some General Criteria for Picking a Meeting Room

While the all-purpose meeting room does not exist, the room selected should meet both physical and psychological requirements of comfort and serviceability. Surroundings tend to effect the way we think and act and a poorly arranged and uncomfortable room is not likely to produce positive meeting results.

Generally speaking, the room should be appropriate to the size of the group. Too small a room is bad, both psychologically and physically. Ventilation is poor, the room gets stuffy, and there is insufficient room in which to move around and set up displays. If the room is too big, the acoustics are likely to be poor. The attendees get a lost, drafty feeling.

Rooms with windows should be avoided if possible and if unavoidable, they should be draped or the chairs faced away from them to avoid outside distractions. Chairs should be comfortable and not crowded together. Opposing groups should not be seated opposite each other as though to invite battle. Members who tend to form obstruction groups should not be seated together but interspersed around the room to give the meeting leader more effective control.

If permanent meeting rooms are to be set aside, long narrow rooms should be avoided. They do not make it convenient to group the audience close to the speaker. They do not enable the audience to face each other comfortably for cross-discussion purposes.

Obstructing posts or columns which interfere with the visibility either of the speaker or of members of the group should be avoided or minimized. The speaker should be in a slightly elevated position where everyone can see him and he can see all of the participants.

The needs of visual display should be kept in mind in view of the growing use of visual communications aids. Electrical outlets should be located near the head of the table, to permit plugging in any equipment used by the speaker. The outlets should be checked in advance to determine whether they are in proper working order. If audio visual equipment is to be used, it too should be selected in advance and checked for good working condition. If a film projector is to be used, proper space should be selected for it. The screen should be mounted high enough so that those in the rear of the room can see over the heads of those up front. If the meeting is held in a public place, union requirements should be checked to see if the projector can be operated by someone who is not a union member.

Obviously, the room should have adequate lighting but it also should have provisions for darkening the room if it is necessary to show films, slides or video tape. Electric outlets should be checked to determine if they are operable when the room is darkened. In the case of projection of overhead transparencies, darkening the room will not be necessary as the transparencies show up very well even in a lighted room.

Room acoustics are important. Bouncing sound waves soon get on the nerves of speakers and listeners. They interfere with listening comfort beyond relatively short periods. You can check room acoustics by clapping your hands together sharply. Poor acoustics will produce a brittle, ringing echo. The real test of how sound carries is to listen when a room is filled with people. Acoustic properties are improved by full attendance. Anything you can do to soften hard surfaces will cut down on bouncing sound. This includes draping the walls, carpeting the floor, and finishing walls and ceilings with acoustic tiles. Audiences which cannot hear soon cease to listen.

It is important to limit room access in order to minimize disturbances from people who arrive late, or who must leave while the meeting is in process. Access should ordinarily be from the rear of the room. When there are two or more entrances to a meeting room, usually only one should be used, with the other closed off. Incoming telephone calls should not be permitted to interrupt meeting proceedings. They should be intercepted by a secretary for later delivery. All attempts should be made to avoid distracting outside noises from faulty plumbing, noisy elevators or other meetings.

Restroom facilities should be readily available, their location known by the participants and ample time allowed for their use during breaks or an emergency.

Checkroom facilities also should be provided for storing of coats, packages, cameras, etc., to avoid cluttering up the meeting room. If coffee breaks are permitted, they should be held close to the meeting room to avoid undue tardiness in returning to the meeting.

Whether one is speaking of an annual conference attended by a large audience or the simplest of all gatherings—the daily business meeting involving a handful of men in an office—visual aids can improve the communicating process. In this photo a team of marketing specialists review a new training program with the aid of a 3M Model 5-088 portable overhead projector.

Needless to say, liquor should not be permitted at any meeting unless called for by some unusual management strategy.

Finally, there is the matter of adequate ventilation. A combination of body heat and smoke will soon make people uncomfortable, thereby interfering with the meeting itself. Unless you have a no smoking rule, you must make sure that there is a sufficient intake of fresh air to expel the hot, stale air at a sufficiently rapid rate. An electric fan in a closed room is not sufficient. It merely recirculates the stale air without replenishing it. Even though you have an air conditioning system, you might still have to open doors and windows occasionally to get a massive replacement of air. This can be done during a coffee break.

The Office as Meeting Center

If anyone made a survey, chances are it would find that most meetings are conducted in regular private offices. If the office has a conference table, this is an advantage. Otherwise the meeting participants gather in a semi-circle around the desk of the person who calls the meeting.

How much can be accomplished in this type of environment? And how much *cannot?*

One possible difficulty is in not having enough room for visual displays and projections. Even this can be remedied by keeping one light-painted wall free of obstructions. Then you can project directly on the wall. If you want to get a little fancier, with much better image display, you can hang a pull-down screen on the ceiling or wall. The overhead projector is well suited to the average office because the room does not have to be darkened, while the image itself is of generous size.

The size of the meeting group and the purpose of the meeting largely determine the best room arrangement. Improper arrangements can destroy the affectiveness of the meeting.

There are four basic arrangements that have survived the test of time and thousands of meetings. Properly used they will enable you to plan your meeting creatively. The diagrams that follow show these basic arrangements and, in addition, the best way in which to position audiovisual equipment for use with each arrangement.

Often the objectives of your meeting will dictate the necessity of having both a large room in which the entire audience can be assembled for opening remarks, lectures and major presentations and, later, smaller rooms for intimate discussions and workshops. It would be best to have the four, five or six rooms necessary to accomplish this, but there are times when one large room must suffice. Properly divided it can be made to do so.

Typical Meeting Room Arrangements

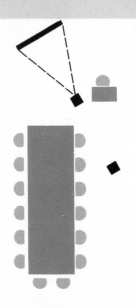

Center table arrangement
Suitable for under 20 people. Promotes discussion. Best for long meetings.

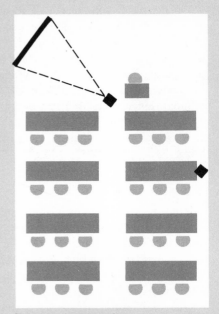

Classroom arrangement
Suitable for any size audience.

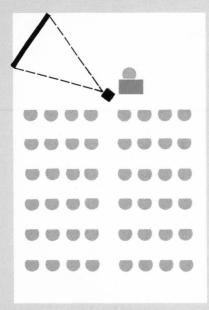

Auditorium or theater arrangement
Suitable for any size audience.

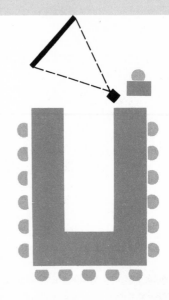

U-Table arrangement
Suitable for 30 people or less. Promotes discussion.

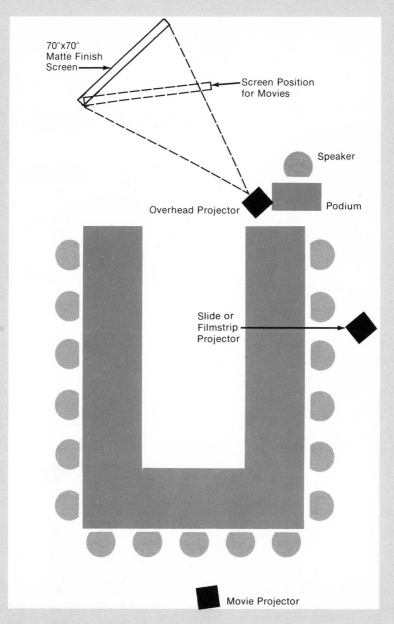

70"x70" Matte Finish Screen

Screen Position for Movies

Speaker

Overhead Projector

Podium

Slide or Filmstrip Projector

Movie Projector

Best for discussion meetings and groups of 30 people or less.

Horizontal Work Table Arrangement

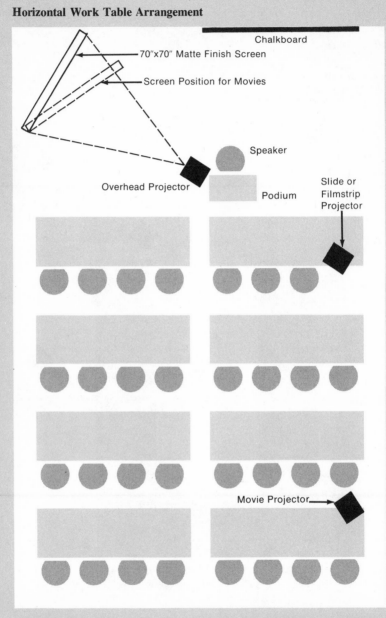

Chalkboard
70"x70" Matte Finish Screen
Screen Position for Movies
Speaker
Overhead Projector
Podium
Slide or Filmstrip Projector
Movie Projector

Suitable arrangement for any size group. Good for work-lecture combination groups of 15-100 people. Projection of screen size increases in larger rooms. Ceiling height should increase accordingly. Best for dissemination of information and for meetings at which little discussion is expected or desired

I recall a particular meeting in which the use of one room for two specific purposes proved ideal. Our goal was to introduce a new product and a new marketing concept to more than 100 persons, then have each person practice using the product in four major applications. Our answer was to set up the room for a presentation to the entire group in the morning, then set up four separate corner workshops, each concentrating on a single application, in the afternoon. We then divided our group into four workshop groups of 25 each and rotated these groups through the four workshops.

Little effort was involved in setting up the individual workshops since the equipment used already was in the room. As a side benefit, keeping everyone on their feet and moving helped combat the drowsy feeling that so often follows a meal. This was good meeting planning at its best and it paid off in results.

The use of folding doors or other room dividers that may be available is another way to separate a single large meeting group into smaller working groups. Many dividers are soundproof and, if these are used, talks may be given simultaneously in the divided areas. If possible, of course, speakers should stand at opposite ends of the larger room to reduce any possible distraction. This, too, is good meeting planning.

The diagram on page 50 shows four possible ways in which to use a single large room first set up for a classroom-type lecture, then in three other ways.

Equipment for the Meeting Room

We can divide meeting rooms into two main types: the large meeting room—sometimes approaching auditorium size—and the permanent meeting or conference room in which activity is built around a conference table. Each must be equipped somewhat differently since the primary function of each is somewhat different.

Equipping the Larger Room

In the larger meeting room, most activity centers around the speaker's table. The audience typically is seated on chairs facing the speaker's

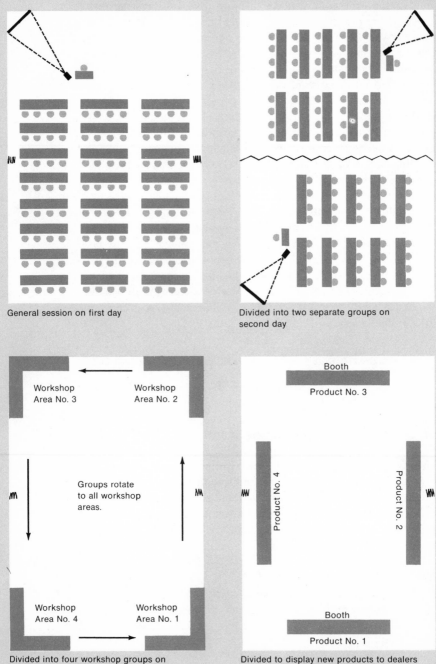

General session on first day

Divided into two separate groups on second day

Workshop Area No. 3

Workshop Area No. 2

Groups rotate to all workshop areas.

Workshop Area No. 4

Workshop Area No. 1

Divided into four workshop groups on third day

Booth

Product No. 3

Product No. 4

Product No. 2

Booth

Product No. 1

Divided to display new products to dealers and outside groups on fourth day table or stand. The permanently installed equipment for such a room would include:

1. Speaker's table and lectern
2. Microphone hook-up
3. Wall- or ceiling-mounted screen.
4. At least two easels, one of which should be of the roller type, suitable for large displays.
5. Necessary projection equipment.
6. One or more small tables on which to put speakers' presentation materials.
7. Chairs for speakers.

Except in the very large meeting rooms, an optional arrangement is to have audience seats which are not fixed to the floor. This permits rearranging chairs for small discussion groups. Sometimes you may want to subdivide a meeting into what are called *buzz groups* permitting more intimate discussion among fewer people, who then report back to the meeting.

If motion pictures are to be projected, you will need either a projection room for the permanent auditorium or a suitable projection table with convenient access to an electrical outlet.

Equipping the Ordinary Conference Room

The ordinary conference room should be equipped with:

1. Overhead projector and wall-mounted or pull-down screen.
2. At least two easels, one of which should be of the roller type, on which to mount large displays.
3. Small cabinet-tables in which to store supplies.
4. Blackboard.
5. Pads, pencils, blackboard eraser, chalk, easel pads, crayons, ash trays, water glasses, water pitchers, etc.

The conference table deserves special mention. Sometimes you see a diagram of ideal conference arrangements which shows people grouped around a circular table. How many such tables have you seen since the round, pedestal-based dining room table went out of vogue? In elegant board rooms they have been replaced, in many instances, by long tables that bulge out at the middle. These are designed to permit people along the sides to see each other as well as the speaker.

The garden-variety of conference room is equipped with conventional rectangular conference tables. In a small conference room, a table about 6 feet wide makes it possible for people to see each other and still have enough working space for their papers and note pads. More people are accommodated by adding tables side by side or lengthwise. Another arrangement is to place three tables in the shape of a T. As the room gets bigger, you can arrange four tables in the shape of an H. Some people prefer a U-shaped arrangement. Just remember that the further you depart from face-to-face concentration, the less intimate will be the meeting.

Here is a simple chart showing at a glance the most appropriate equipment—graded for effectiveness—for some specific kinds of meetings:

	16 mm	35 mm	Prepared Chart	Blackboard	Easel Pad	Overhead Projector	Desk Projector
Informal Office Meeting				A	A	B	A
Staff Meeting			C	B	A	A	A
Project Review			A	C	C	A	A
Committee Meeting			C	A	A	A	A
Sales Meeting	A	A				A	B
Information Meeting	A	A				A	C
Remote Presentation	A	A				A	C
Annual Convention	A	A	A			A	

Setting Up the Meeting

When meetings are to be held outside your own office, always check out the meeting room. This becomes particularly important when displays have to be set up beforehand. Sometimes an important piece of equipment is missing. If a meeting room is used by others, it is well to verify beforehand that the room has remained available and that it has not been usurped by someone else without your knowledge. Even though meeting rooms are frequently kept under assignment control, some people who pride themselves on being able to get things done without red tape have a way of moving in on the rooms without having reserved them.

All physical arrangements should be checked by one person who, preferably, should work from a written checklist. If you use more than one person, each may assume that the other has checked on some arrangement. Following is a checklist of meeting arrangements:

1. Display media
   a. Projection screens
   b. Blackboard: clean? chalk? erasers?
   c. Easel: set up and in good condition? easel pads? crayons or other markers?
2. Projection equipment
   a. Plugged in and tested?
   b. Focused, framed, and leveled, using actual materials?
   c. Spare lamps and fuses?
   d. Lenses clean?
3. Extension cords in place so that no one will trip over them.
4. Sound equipment installed and tested with loudspeaker in place.
5. Exhibits and projection materials; sequences checked.
6. Microphone checked out.
7. Flashlights or pointers for speaker.
8. Place cards for participants.
9. Writing materials, including note pads and pencils.
10. Ash trays, water glasses, water pitchers.
11. Sufficient number of seats, arranged properly.
12. Provision for room-darkening when necessary.

Screen Size

Screen size must be equated to distance between screen and person sitting furthest from the screen. Screen size dictates magnification possible from projector to screen.

Notes

Notes

Notes

Chapter V.

The Skills of Leadership

"I've always found it easier to draw a piece of spaghetti across a plate, then push it." that is the rather homely aphorism a midwestern business manager once used to describe his technique in getting the most productivity out of his employees.

The technique of getting things done is essentially a technique of communication. One of the foremost skills of managerial leadership is that of communicating effectively. And it is those companies who have developed skillful meeting leaders who are the successful ones.

Almost every football fan on occasion has witnessed an ordinarily superb ball carrier upended behind his line because someone got the signals mixed up. Understandable. If those on a team are given the wrong signals they can hardly be expected to correctly perform their assignments and it is therefore unlikely the play will prove a success.

Elementary, to be sure. But it is the elementary that is so often neglected perhaps because it seems so obvious.

The analogy of the gridiron mix-up applies to the conduct of business too. It is at the business meeting where the conference leader calls all of those involved in an endeavor together to discuss the company game plan and generate enthusiasm and commitment to it. Does everyone clearly know the goal? Does everyone know their roles and assignments? Are we all agreed upon the best plan? What are the problems and how are we going to overcome them? And so on.

The late President Eisenhower once said, "Leadership is the art of getting someone else to do something that you want done because he wants to do it."

Implicit in Mr. Eisenhower's words is the kind of leadership that has achieved effective communication.

Let's think about that one for a moment. If you're running a meeting from a tight agenda and you're clicking all the way, driving home your points and getting the meeting to go along with you, you may be running a meeting, but you may not really be accomplishing much. You could probably get the same effect putting the meeting on a tape beforehand and letting your secretary play it to the group.

On the other hand, if you approach the same meeting with a set of goals in mind, and if you stimulate group discussion that produces good conclusions — perhaps the very conclusions you had in mind — your achievement will have dual value. You will have gained your immediate program while enabling the other participants to feel that they have made significant contributions.

The difference is in technique. You can force through your own views with sledge-hammer tactics, seeming to win support — but winning only resentment. Or you can provide the opportunity for creation of a real group product.

In reference to this point, I am reminded of something purported to have been said by Benjamin Franklin: "If you state an opinion dogmatically which is in direct oppostion to my thought and you imply no room for negotiation, then I must conclude in order to protect my own self-esteem that you are wrong and I will immediately undertake to prove you wrong.

"On the other hand, if you state your opinion as a hypothesis with evidence of a willingness to discuss and explore, I will like as not undertake to prove you correct."

There are specific techniques for encouraging group productivity. These vary with the over-all purpose of the meeting, as well as with innumerable circumstances unique to each company and its key people. Here we will cover some of the basics from the standpoint of the meeting leader. In subsequent chapters, some important variations will be treated.

There are some general guidelines that a conference leader should keep in mind about his role in the meeting:

1. He should know his audience and anticipate participant attitudes and positions.

2. He should speak their language and appeal to their interests.

3. He should organize his materials before hand and know precisely what he wants to say.

4. He should present his materials simply and concisely, using visual aids to enhance his communication.

5. He should present his case in a firm, confident, enthusiastic and well-modulated voice.

6. He should avoid distracting mannerisms of presentation.

7. He should be prepared to consider suggestions and opinions pertinent to the matter under discussion and stimulate group discussion.

Meeting Management

Apart from its content, certain procedures in running a meeting may make the difference between success and failure. These are the businesslike aspects of physically preparing for a meeting, opening it on time, disciplining its course, and closing it on a constructive note. The man who masters these seemingly minor skills draws favorable attention to himself. Because meetings are so often regarded as wastefully time-consuming, the man who wins a reputation forrunning a good show puts himself in a favorable light.

Pre Meeting Activities

The meeting leader who has done a good job of working up the agenda will thereby have simplified the actual setting up of the meeting itself. When he enters the meeting room, he will have a plan of action. Since he will have prearranged for any necessary personnel or informational resources, he is not likely to have to interrupt the meeting to send out for people or documents. He will, of course, have checked on visual aids, special materials, equipment, invited speakers, and any other physical details.

Running the Meeting

A bugaboo of most meetings is the people who arrive late. The meeting chairman must decide quickly whether to delay a half-dozen people for ten or fifteen minutes — representing an hour or an hour and a half of their collective time — or to proceed without the participation of a key person. Although sometimes the key person is so "key" you can't really go ahead, in most cases you should proceed without the late-comer.

Some people are occasionally tardy by inadvertence, but there are others who are chronically late. Waiting for the habitual late-comer is not likely to cure him, but starting without him may make him sufficiently conspicuous so that the next time he may not be late, especially if you take up something before he arrives in which he has an interest.

The way you open a meeting often has a great deal to do with the tone of the whole proceedings. In your opening remarks, you set a climate. It can be positive or negative. It can stimulate people to want to burst forth with ideas or it can drive them into their respective shells. The good leader opens on a positive note even when the occasion scarcely calls for optimism.

Someone needs to take notes. This can be the chairman himself or, when he expects to be actively engaged in discussion, he might have a secretary present or someone who is a participant but does not have the initial burden of chairmanship.

Then there is the matter of the timetable. The chairman knows that he has a certain amount of ground to cover. With one eye on his watch and the other on his agenda, he moves discussion along a little more actively whenever he feels that the action is lagging or that further discussion on a particular matter will be to no avail. Sometimes he must decide that an agenda topic needs to be tabled because there will not be ample time to cover it suitably. This may be a personal judgment if he feels this is within his authority, yet it is something on which he can also seek group assent.

If the meeting is a long one, the chairman will interrupt for a coffee break or a seventh-inning stretch. This can be a strategic interruption which can either be hastened or postponed, depending upon the tenor of the discussion. A short intermission can sometimes be used as a means of heading off a clash. It can also be used for private counseling or sentiment-seeking.

The intermission may occasionally be used as a means of getting around a security problem, such as when you have privileged information to discuss with only some of the participants. During the break you can convene the smaller group privately.

Closing the Meeting

Every meeting should close on some note of positive accomplishment. There is nothing more frustrating than having participants go away muttering among themselves about another hour lost. Although the matter of accomplishment is determined during the course of the meeting, unless it is brought out as a final conclusion or summary, the overall impression may be inconclusive.

If any decisions were reached, these should be restated by the chairman, preferably in precise terms. One effective technique, using an overhead projector, is for the chairman to write out the decision on a sheet of transparency film and project it on the wall or a screen. Anyone who differs with the decision can then state his interpretation.

In addition to decisions, there may be assignments to various participants, as well as to people who are not present. These also should be reiterated. Each person present who is affected might be asked to state his due-date, although sometimes this must be worked out collectively when there is some form of team action to be taken.

A training or informational meeting might not require restatement of decisions and specific assignments, yet here also one can end on a positive note. The chairman should summarize what has been accomplished. He might relate his summary to the future work assignments and goals of the participants. He might also indicate what is to be taken up next in a series of related meetings.

Leadership Behavior

Meeting leaders are not born; they are made. At least this is true of good meeting leaders. One of the cardinal sins of most chairmen and leaders is that they talk too much, according to Dr. Alfred J. Marrow, author of *Making Management Human*. He told of a study which revealed that the average leader took 60 per cent of the conference time. None of the meeting leaders in this study group clocked less than 30 per cent. In one instance, the figure was 92 per cent. Contrast this with a rule of thumb that no meeting leader should take more than 20 per cent of the meeting time!

On the assumption that most meeting leaders would be eager to reform if they could see themselves as others do, we will next examine some typical faults of meeting chairmen and leaders. There is a slight distinction between the two. Sometimes you, as a participant, are called upon to make a presentation or to lead a discussion within the meeting.

For that purpose, you have also become an *ad hoc* meeting leader. Hence, this part of the chapter is for both regular chairmen and participants.

Podium Pointers

The podium can be a speaker's effective tool for making points and creating a "Now hear this" atmosphere — or it can be the biggest menace a presenter of ideas can have. The chances are that each of us is guilty of some of the following practices. As you read, try to recognize yourself. Perhaps you fit into no single category but are guilty of a malpractice here and there. What is important is the *overuse* of any of the podium practices that will now be caricatured. The serious point is that they distract the members of the audience and detract from your personal dignity.

The *gripper* looks as if he were standing on the side of a mountain. The only thing keeping him from tumbling over is the podium onto which he is hanging for dear life. If he is nervous, he may gain sympathy, but not much else. If you're the gripper type, remember that the more relaxed you can appear, the more relaxed and receptive your audience will be. They will feel you have command over your subject matter and will win their confidence. The gripper should always remember that the best of performers comes on stage feeling a little nervous. There are innumerable tales of great actors who confess with humility to this common attribute. One technique that might succeed for you is to forget that you are talking to a roomful of people. Instead, concentrate on speaking to one person at a time, even looking him in the eye. Pretend that you are having a man-to-man talk.

The *musician* has the habit of nervously rattling coins or keys in his pocket distracting the audience, particularly those up front. The jingling competes with his message. (In truth, any mannerism is distracting.) Remember the steel balls that Captain Queeg of *The Caine Mutiny* clicked and clacked in his hand? If this is one of your faults, there is a simple cure. Remove coins, keys and steel balls from your pockets before you get up in front of the group.

The *weakling* relaxes by leaning on the podium. You get the feeling he would fall if you pulled the podium out from under him. Crouched over, he cramps his own chest cavity and cannot sound out with strength and vigor. The audience tends to impute weakness to his ideas and messages. Maybe this type of speaker needs to get a little more sleep the night before, but chances are, he would improve it if he were simply made conscious of his fault.

Today the *orator* is seldom able to manipulate captive audiences as did the great Mark Antony. There are times and places for spellbinding speeches. You make a brief one in the football locker room before you charge the men to victory. You make a speech for posterity if you address Congress at a time of national crisis. But the occasion for old-fashioned full-throated oratory is not the business meeting. The "spellbinder" soon becomes boring; he tends to make his listeners feel he is talking down to them.

The *pacer* is a cross between Roger Bannister in the midst of an early morning work-out and a caged lion — always on the move, realizing there is no escape. The pacer has got to be well prepared, or at least well versed in his subject matter, since he never gets close enough to the podium to follow his notes! He may actually overlook important points he had planned to make. The audience tends to focus on his acrobatics instead of his words.

The *bon voyageur* is the man who just took his millionaire mother-in-law down to the ship for a cruise to Europe. He just can't wave goodbye fast enough or hard enough! Limited hand gesturing can lend emphasis when a speaker stands before a fairly large group; overuse is a distraction.

The *reader* has his nose buried in his notes. He may resort to the written word either because he is ill-prepared or because he does not have sufficient confidence in himself. How does the audience feel about it? The listeners — if they can hear the words directed toward the sheet of paper — are likely to feel that if he didn't consider it important enough to be better prepared, why should they think it important enough to listen?

Although we have found fault with each of the characters just described, there is a happy combination which takes the best from each one of them — except the musician and the reader. A good speaker varies his presentation. He avoids monotony. Because he knows his subject, he convinces the audience that he believes in it. To command attention he borrows something from the gripper and the orator for special emphasis, or from the bon voyageur, with an occasional gesture.

If you want to stimulate participation and free discussion, you may want to create a relaxed atmosphere by occasionally leaning on the podium in a chummy way or even sitting on a chair on the same level as the group. You can put the audience at ease by sitting on the edge of the table.

For an occasional change of pace, to break the spell of an audience whose eyes are riveted on one spot, you can cross from one side to the other briefly and return to the podium.

The point is, you can use the best of the foregoing in good taste. It is only the extremes that becomes offensive.

These podium pointers also apply to the conventional business meeting that is carried out around the conference table.

A Glossary of Deadly Sins

The chairman often commits other sins that detract from his personal effectiveness and also from the accomplishment of his meeting goals; search your soul for these:

1. Do you hog the meeting, not giving anyone else a chance to contribute an independent thought? If you do, the net result of your efforts will be resentment. In the eyes of the group members, you become Mr. Autocrat. In seeming not to care about the views of others, you take away from their dignity. How could they not be resentful?

2. Do you come to a meeting ill-prepared, taking up topics that someone has put together for you? Do you shuffle through supporting papers, nervously seeking catchwords and clues to the subject matter you're supposed to lead in discussion? If so, you will be as transparent as the professor who comes to a lecture without advance preparation. The meeting will ramble while you fumble. You will waste the time of all those present and they will resent this waste.

3. Do you let the meeting run away by itself, off schedule, as though it were a train without a motorman or conductor? Do you patiently wait while each person exhausts himself with his own remarks before you recognize someone else? Do you wind up the meeting an hour late, without apparent accomplishment, or do you wind up on time with even less done?

4. Do you resent questions or comments from the participants which seem to challenge something you say? Do you convey the impression that unless your word is taken as law there will be retaliations and recriminations? You will be resented by all present and the blow to their morale cannot help but carry over to their work outside the meeting room itself. You are destroying initiative. If it persists, it will be in spite of you, probably out of a sense of greater loyalty to the company itself!

5. Are you a comic? Do you feel that you must tell funny stories and off-color jokes? A funny story that has good content will occasionally relieve tensions and help put across a key point, but too much of a good thing can deprive a meeting of its tone of serious business.

6. Do you publicly chastise members of the group? Do you pick on specific individuals and subject them to harassment or ridicule?

Even if you seem to be doing it in jest, your behavior will be resented. Save your criticisms for a private conference.

7. Do you permit interruptions? Every time you take a mid-conference telephone call, you are using up the time of all the other people present. The same goes for letters, memoranda, or other documents brought in to you during the course of a meeting for your perusal while others cool their heels. If you're running a meeting specify for your secretary the *emergency* conditions that warrant interruption.

Tips on Meeting Management

Books and articles that tell you how to run good meetings will sometimes include checklists of the personality characteristics of meeting chairmen. They are very interesting. They are also out of this world! Their fallacy is in taking all of the best out of past, present, and future meeting chairmen. Sometimes, by contrast, they also have checklists of inadequate chairmen. Usually, the truth lies somewhere in between.

The trouble with these checklists is that they ignore the realities of business life. People are asked to take over the chairmanship of meetings because they are in supervisory or executive positions or for a variety of other reasons having little to do with someone's checklist of the attributes of a good chairman. It is much more important that we concentrate on improving performance of each person who actually chairs a meeting than that we look for the ideal chairman in the first place.

The Meeting in the Stream of Management

A meeting is a juncture in the stream of management activity. When used to achieve a particular objective, it becomes an important management tool. The chairman approaches each new meeting conscious of this overall stream of activity, to which he must relate the discussions and accomplishments of the meeting about to take place. The meeting must fit into the overall scheme of his superiors. It must take into account the activities and requirements of other segments of the organization — perhaps to be governed by them or perhaps to take a position which will properly attempt to change the others.

What goes on in the meeting must also be related to the chairman's own overall activity scheme. He must keep in mind his future as well as his present work goals.

In short, the meeting is not a gathering of and by itself. It may result in a specific achievement and yet have widespread repercussions and ramifications. It may be one of a series of meetings, each of which lays the ground for a succeeding one. All of this strategic overhead must be kept in mind by the chairman.

How to Coax a Meeting Along

With a little practice, you can learn to keep a discussion moving along briskly. There is nothing so deadly as a meeting that gets stalled either for ideas or for not bringing matters to a head. Such a meeting marks the chairman as ineffective.

Here are seven control points for the chairman. You might write them on a 3'' x 5'' card and glance at it privately during the meeting as a self-reminder. After awhile, you'll get to know the points by heart.

1. Stimulate discussion; don't let it lag.
2. Balance the discussion; don't let any single point of view predominate when others are to be heard.
3. Keep the discussion on track; don't let people digress.
4. Break up hot controversies; they'll tear the meeting apart.
5. Keep the meeting lively; don't let people daydream.
6. Watch your timetable; finish on schedule.
7. Make sure there is a conclusion and some positive action initiated.

To *stimulate discussion* you may have to do little more than announce the topic, particularly if there are people champing at the bit to have their say. Often, however, you must start the ball rolling. You might start with a general question addressed to the group, inviting a response. If this doesn't work, you might make the next question more specific, addressing it to a particular person. To assure that discussion takes place on particularly important topics, I personally would not hesitate to brief one of the participants in advance so that he asks certain questions or raises specific points. Or, perhaps all you need do is call on someone who has been assigned a discussion topic. At any rate, don't phrase questions so as to elicit a straight *yes* or *no*.

To *balance discussions*, you must have done some homework beforehand. You have to know the issues and you have to know the people and their viewpoints. Then, if the discussion gets one-sided, you turn to someone who can balance it off. If someone hogs the floor, you tune your ear for a cue in one of his remarks that will permit you to interrupt him. Then, cut your own brief remarks short and turn the discussion over to someone else.

To *avoid digressions*, you might just tell the group when a subject is off the official topic. If you need to be more gentle, you can pick up the discussion from the digressing speaker and then turn it back to the scheduled topic, perhaps by calling on someone to respond to a point that you raise. You might restate the issues or the meeting purpose and relate the ongoing discussion accordingly.

To *break up controversy*, you might call a short recess, or this may be the moment for a suitable anecdote. The chairman is also privileged to get into the discussion long enough to take it away from the parties in controversy. If you then bring in someone else, those who have been arguing will have an opportunity to cool off — but don't discourage spirited discussion on a friendly and constructive basis.

To *keep the meeting alive*, bounce around the ball of discussion. If you see someone daydreaming or fidgeting, find an excuse to get him into the act. The fault may also be your own. If so, liven up the proceedings by changing your pace, telling an appropriate anecdote, putting something on an overhead projector as a means of stimulating discussion, walking over to a chalkboard, and in any other way stimulating a little action.

To *get through the agenda*, keep each topic or subtopic to its allotted span of time. Work toward the key issues. Sacrifice the details if you are on a tight schedule. If you have to cut discussion short, break into it with some relevant point that will enable you to tie the speaker's comments into a further statement by you of the understandings or agreements reached up to that point.

Reaching a conclusion and initiating positive action should be the end to your meeting. Never leave the meeting room proud that you finished the agenda if you didn't state a conclusion, summarize your results or get action started on the new business you decided in the meeting.

Meeting in Stereo

This is a new technique — rapidly growing in popularity — that is worth a try. It is called "meeting in stereo" because two speakers are in front of the audience at the same time.

The two may comment alternately or may carry on a controlled discussion which can include the audience. The result is a fast-paced presentation which is almost certain to keep the attention of the audience.

While it can be made to work with any visual aid, the meeting in stereo is primarily designed for use with the overhead projector (or two overhead projectors) because of the projector's flexibility. The projector must be speaker operated; the speaker will project visuals as the pace of the meeting requires, and in most cases will add spontaneous, or apparently spontaneous, remarks to the visuals.

We have used this technique when we wished to talk about one specific subject from two points of view. Examples are meetings in stereo conducted by a sales manager and a technical manager, or a design engineer and a production engineer.

This technique is most effective when it is well rehearsed yet appears spontaneous. There is great advantage in losing the rigidity of audience-speaker relationship. Meetings in stereo encourage discussion. The diagram on the opposite page shows a typical room arrangement for a meeting in stereo.

Bar Stool Technique

The use of a bar stool as a prop at business meetings — rather than as a place for business meetings — establishes an easy, relaxed way to communicate. Perched on a stool in front of his audience, either beside or behind a podium or without a podium, the speaker immediately establishes a kind of informal rapport with his audience. He sets the tone for business to come, creates a mood for active discussion and, at the same time, leaves himself free to get up and move about on occasion, most often to add emphasis to his remarks.

There is another benefit in the use of the bar stool: often speakers who find themselves inclined to tense up while standing before an audience find the mere act of sitting down to talk relaxes them — and produces a better talk.

One final point, these are techniques, tested and found useful, but still techniques. Techniques improve with rehearsal. In short — rehearse, rehearse, rehearse and rehearse again. "Unaccustomed as I am to public speaking" is a description that fits most of us. So, rehearse. Know your talk, your presentation, whatever it is you wish to say, so well that you can concentrate, not on what you must say, but on how well you can say it.

Some Problem Participants

The problem characters for whom the chairman must be on the alert are three: the show-stealers, the disrupters, and the blackouts.

Show-stealers are usually talkative types who want to make a big

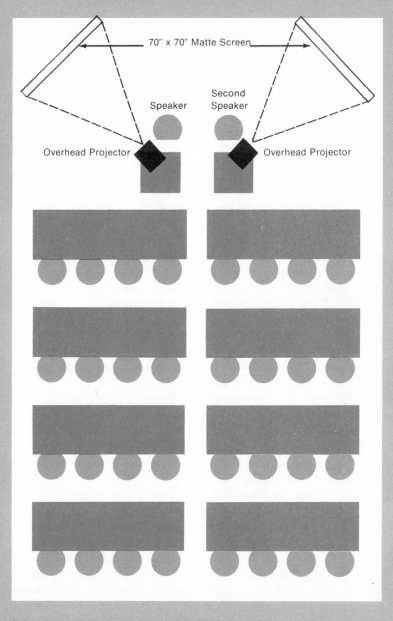

Suitable for any size group—two speakers. Both speakers may remain at projector positions for skit or question-answer type presentation or one may move off while the other takes over the presentation.

impression but have little to contribute, or get started and then do not know how to stop.

The talker who has little to say is a relatively simple problem. The chairman spots him as a nuisance and learns to bypass him in recognizing others who have something worthwhile to contribute. Occasionally, he can be omitted from a meeting. This might tip him off. There's also no substitute for a good, private, supervisory discussion. A little more delicate problem is represented by the man who has a great deal to contribute but tends to do so at the expense of others' opportunities. The supervisory treatment must be handled delicately. In the meeting itself, the chairman will feel that he cannot afford to cut off worthwhile discussion, but he must strive to recognize others and to cut the talkative one short, once he has made his key point.

The *disrupters* fall into these subcategories: rude persons, hecklers, and recalcitrants.

Rude participants may be talking on the side or doing independent paperwork. The best approach probably is to address specific questions to them for comment.

The several varieties of heckler may have deep-seated psychological problems. Their complaints may pertain to the office or to situations at home. The chairman' should avoid open chastisement. He should pick up and restate objections or criticisms raised by the heckler and turn these over to the group itself for disposal. If the heckler continues to be disruptive, chances are the group will dispose of him. He will be regarded collectively as a threat.

Recalcitrants are somewhat different. These are people who are rigidly committed to a particular viewpoint. The chairman can raise questions which bring in other sides of the problem. He can also pass the ball to other members of the meeting group for them to press contrasting viewpoints. Beyond these efforts, the meeting can do little more but express its own consensus.

The *blackouts* are those who do not participate. They may have contributions to make, but for reasons unknown, sometimes even to themselves, they are reluctant to express themselves. They perhaps consider it safer to keep their own counsel or they may feel insecure about expressing their thoughts. Sometimes they may actually have nothing to say. The chairman should try to draw any of these people into discussion when he has an idea they have a worthwhile contribution to make not yet expressed. Merely drawing them into discussion for the sake of participation can embarrass them. The chairman should be alert to logical opportunities to seek the comments of opinions of these noncommunicative types.

Summary:

Remember that the business meeting is a vital communications tool which all successful companies have assiduously developed. It is at the meeting that the company game plan is outlined, the signals made clear, roles and assignments clearly defined, problems discovered and overcome. It is the meeting leader who recognizes this tool for what it is and develops himself into the expert meeting communicator so necessary to his and his company's success and growth. Here are some do's and don'ts to guide the meeting leader:

Do's

1. Semper Paratus. Always prepare your materials and meeting room arrangements beforehand. Know precisely what you want to say.
2. Know your audience and anticipate participant attitudes and positions.
3. Speak their language and appeal to their interests.
4. Present your materials simply and concisely, using visual aids to enhance communication.
5. Be firm, confident, enthusiastic and speak in a clear voice.
6. Consider participants' suggestions and opinions and stimulate group discussion.
7. Take a break if meeting is a long one.
8. Keep the discussion balanced. Stimulate when necessary.
9. Open and close the meeting promptly.
10. Close the meeting on a note of accomplishment and make sure the decisions reached are clear to everyone.

Don'ts

1. Avoid distracting physical mannerisms in presentation.
2. Don't attempt to lead a meeting without preparation.
3. Don't hog the meeting, preventing others from participating.
4. Lead at all times. Don't let the meeting drift or digress.
5. Avoid show of resentment to a challenge of your own ideas.
6. Don't use humor in poor taste.
7. Don't subject anyone to harassment or ridicule.
8. Don't let hot controversies develop.
9. Don't let the meeting become dull, putting people to sleep.

Notes

Chapter VI

The Skills of Participation

What's in it for me?

Some version or other of that question is probably one of the most often asked questions in the field of daily commerce. There perhaps is no better determination of whether there has been effective communication than a determination of whether you have satisfactorily answered that query to those whom you are trying to convince.

In terms of both company and individual business success (which should be inextricably inter-twined) the answer to that question in relationship to skillful meeting participation is simply: success.

Just as there is a direct, observable relationship between the successful, growing companies and those who have developed effective internal communications so there is a direct relationship between individual success and those who can effectively lead and participate (communicate) in the business meeting. One need not belabor the obvious point that the most important ingredient in a company is not the bricks and mortar but people.

It is interesting to note in this respect the origin of the word "company." It derives the medieval English term, "compaigne," then to an earlier and similar French word and finally back to the Latin word, "companio," all of which meant, simply, companion or companionship.

In other words, "company" originally meant, not a master-slave nor boss-subordinate relationship but a gathering together of companions who had an interest in working together to achieve a common goal.

There must be leadership of course. It is also interesting to note that leadership means just that. To lead, direct, guide. Not push, confuse, threaten or intimidate.

But companions working together have to talk together, communicate together if they are going to successfully determine where they want to go and how they are going to get there.

And it is in the business meeting where the seeds of business success are planted, where the members get together, communicate, coordinate, align efforts and reach agreement on common purpose.

What's in it for those who master the skills of meeting participation? Both individual, and therefore, company success.

Specialization is one of the most important characteristics of modern management. Subdivision of tasks and assignments to individual executives and technical specialists creates a continuing challenge to management: how to coordinate all of this effort most effectively in the achievement of common goals.

As much as we all talk we often find it difficult to understand each other. Some people communicate well. Mastery of a few simple techniques has helped them toward success. If you look about you, you will note that the topmost executives have certain attributes in common. They may have started as engineers, salesmen, accountants, production planners, or personnel specialists — to mention just a few — but by the time they get to the top they have acquired certain important personal attributes. They have learned to be highly expressive, mainly in their oral communication, but also in their written communication. If you look further, you will find that they have also learned how to think and talk in total company terms.

There is probably no more effective medium for acquiring these skills than participation in management conferences.

Your Stake in Participation

As a participant in a management conference, you can benefit three ways: if you're observant and attentive, you can acquire a liberal education in general management; through participation you have a wonderful opportunity to sharpen your knowledge in your own field; and you'll have one of the best opportunities to make your supervisors aware of your personal attributes and potentials. The meeting is actually a two-level medium of personnel development. If your responsibilities call for you to be a chairman, you engage in a direct management experience. At the same time, you participate in the meetings called by your superiors.

Meetings and Your Higher Education

When you sit around the conference table with other men in your own department, you have an excellent means of learning about the total function of the department. When people from other departments come into your meeting, or when you attend an interdepartmental meeting, your continuing management education is broadened considerably. You learn to tie together all of the functional aspects of running a business. You begin to see the other man's point of view. More important, you learn the overall company view. When you reflect this in your own work operations, you eventually become identified as a "company man." If you are personally expressive as well, you may find yourself called upon increasingly to speak for management in a variety of situations.

The business meeting, then, may be described as a continuing seminar, a continuing education, on business management. It is one of the best post-graduate courses you can take.

A Chance to Sharpen

A second aspect of the management meeting is that it offers you an opportunity to sharpen your own knowledge and skills. It is one thing to be able to learn from the performance of others. It is another to go through the experience of preparing well for your own participation. This is the really intensifying experience. It forces you to think *actively*. If you prepare well, you must think about goals, viewpoints of others, resources, and technical problems, to mention a few. Then, when you make your presentation, you have a roomful of critics who will review your thinking and help advance it to the next stage of accomplishment.

A Chance to Shine

Through active participation in management meetings, you have one of the best means for bringing your talents to the attention of your superiors. Instead of having to say outright, "What a great guy am I!" you make it possible for your superiors to draw their own conclusions. If your participation enables them to accomplish goals more readily, you will be observed and remembered favorably. The management meeting is a ready-made vehicle for personal public relations. It is amazing how many people fail to take advantage of it.

Prerequisites to Effective Participation

The ability to shine in a meeting calls for something more than mere determination. You just cannot walk in, sit down, and join in a discussion without the existence of two general prerequisites. One has to do with the climate for participation, the other involves the hard work of detailed preparation.

A Climate for Participation

While this chapter is addressed in the main to the individual participant, it contains a message for management. The ideal is to get each member of the management team to identify his self-interests with those of overall management. Practically speaking, the individual is primarily conscious of the personal opportunities for professional and financial advancement. If he believes that his company is interested in good performance and will give him an opportunity to move ahead, he will find it attractive to merge the company interests with his own.

This calls for a great deal of positive effort. It is an ideal not merely to be spoken of. Rather, it must be ratified routinely in the course of daily interactions. The people of the organization must feel that their ideas are welcomed and that they are given recognition for them. As a corollary to this — and perhaps this is even more important — they must feel that an occasional useless idea will not bring disgrace.

We need to be even more specific. Each employee will seek his own measure of management attitudes. He will find it in the response to his memoranda. He will find it in the way his comments are received in conference discussions. He will watch to see how other employees are treated when they initiate good ideas. If the company has failed to generate a climate for good participation, it will discover its failure in a pervasive attitude which is expressed in a familiar saying, "Don't stick your neck out."

Good participation must be a way of life. It cannot begin and end in the conference room. It calls for doing your assignment as best you can on a day-to-day basis, but in addition it calls for you to think always beyond your assignment. That is, you must be aware of the larger framework of activity of which you are a part. How do you do this? You read company publications and memoranda even though you are not specifically requested to do so. You talk with your colleagues about your mutual problems. You keep up to date in your own professional field through reading professional and trade journals. You might even attend an outside course.

Get into the habit of analysis. Before you take an action think of every conceivable effect of that action on your own work, on that of others in your department, and on the work of other departments. Convert each mistake into a gain by learning what not to do the next time.

Techniques of Active Participation

Thus far we have dealt rather generally with benefits and attitudes of mind. Now we should discuss behavior in the arena of the conference room.

In an earlier chapter on the planning of meetings, we made the point that success depends mainly on the work done before entering the meeting room. The actual conference situation — important as it is — can almost be likened to the visible tip of an iceberg.

For convenience, discussion of the techniques of participation will be divided into two parts: your participation in general, and your participation when you have a direct assignment.

General Tips for Participation

Here are nine tips on conference participation. If you master these, you are bound to acquire a reputation as an ideal conference participant.

1. Never enter a conference room without having done your homework. Acquaint yourself beforehand with the problems, the issues, and the varying points of view pertaining to each topic on the agenda.

When working papers are distributed, read them *before* you come into the conference room.

2. Approach the meeting with an open mind. You may have firm ideas or convictions. You may be enthusiastic about them. You may be 100 percent right — as far as you have gone. You may be wrong in some particulars. Not everyone in the meeting room is going to be right about what he has to say. You could be one of those who is wrong in whole or in part. Your best defense against grievous error is to approach the meeting with a mixture of confidence through knowledge, cautious reservation, and a willingness to consider the viewpoints of others which might be just as enthusiastically presented.

3. Don't shuffle papers or engage in side conversations. You will distract others. You will also convey the impression that you did not come to the meeting well prepared.

4. Your meeting manners should be at least as good as when you entertain in your own home or are a guest in the home of others. When there are differences of opinion, don't personalize them. Respect the views of your colleagues. Don't attack any of them on a personal basis merely because you disagree. Show an active interest in what they have to say and when you agree with them, let them know this. Don't hold back as though you were playing bluff poker.

5. Speak up when you have something to say on which you are knowledgeable. Respect the right of others to get a word or two in edgewise. Don't overdo your participation. If you are well prepared, you might feel an urge to comment extensively, if for no other reason than that others might not be as well prepared. In this case, restrict yourself to the most important and most meaty comments. Your participation will be regarded as having more depth.

6. Listen to what others say. Listen actively. Most people tend to listen to themselves and to think about their own problems while others are talking, unless their self-interest is involved. If you spend even a little effort in listening actively, you will be ahead of most other people! More important, you will learn a great deal.

7. Take lots of notes. This is part of the active learning process. Date your notes and file them, at least temporarily, for they will be valuable sources of reference in case of some later debate about what was or was not said in the meeting. From the more constructive standpoint, note-taking fixes thoughts in one's mind. Also, as others observe you taking notes, they will tend to be more businesslike in their discussions.

8. Don't surprise your own boss with a new proposal you make in a meeting. If you do, you force him either to be quiet or to disavow what you have to say. It is a safer course to discuss your proposals

with him before the meeting. He might tell you to drop them — which is his prerogative — or he might encourage you to present them, even though he is not yet in agreement. At best, you can get his active support for your idea by disclosing it to him in advance.

9. Don't provoke controversy with other participants in a meeting if this can be avoided. If you have done your homework well, you will have a fairly good idea of points of sensitivity and controversy. Although controversy is not to be avoided when it is in the best interests of the company, you might find through some pre-talk that you can accomplish your aims or find honorable and worthwhile retreat while avoiding an explosion.

Handling an Assignment

When you are given a meeting assignment, the spotlight is on you as an active participant. You may be in the role of a persuader, or you might actually take over as meeting leader for the particular topic. If you want a formula that has worked for even the most inexperienced conference participants, here it is:

1. Prepare yourself in depth. Pretend that you are participating in a war game in which you have to plan your moves in the light of what you expect from the opposition. Although you do not look upon your colleagues as the enemy, you regard them as constructive opposition. Anticipate every possible objection or dificulty that might be raised by others. Accept whatever you should with an open mind and be prepared to argue with facts on the rest.

2. Make an outline of your presentation. Prepare this sufficiently in advance so that you will have time to improve upon it.

3. Build your presentation around visuals whenever possible. As a rule of thumb, figure on four visuals for every ten minutes of discussion. Even though you are not an accomplished speaker or ''conference craftsman,'' you can carry off your presentation with a professional quality, if you build around visuals.

4. Rehearse your presentation before you enter the conference room. Do this even though you think you know the subject fully. A rehearsal, *aloud*, either in solo or with others, will unify your presentation and bring out areas for improvement.

5. When your presentation is to lead to a decision, try out your proposals beforehand on key people who will participate in the final decision. They may modify your thinking or you may modify theirs. In either case, you will at least know what you are in for and you may be able to win adherence to your proposals.

6. If you're extremely well prepared, you won't need to write out

a long speech. If you do write it out don't read it. Reading detracts from the feeling that you know your subject well. In fact, if you have a written talk but don't have to refer to it line by line you convey just the opposite impression — to the satisfaction of all concerned. If you are new at the game and speaking before a large group makes you dreadfully nervous, *do* write out your speech. Write the best copy of your life, using easy conversational language. Read it over and over at home out loud (full volume), and keep polishing it word by word and phrase by phrase until it sounds as natural and conversational as you can get it. Commit to memory your opening statement and look your audience dead in the eye as you deliver it. This will give you a running start. You'll pass through the sound barrier of initial nervousness. The rest will be clear sailing. You may never need to read another speech!

I find that key words written on the frame of overhead projection transparencies serve as an excellent means for prompting me during a presentation. In fact, these key words function as an effective outline for my talk.

7. If you don't know your subject or if you are not able to respond to someone's question, don't bluff and don't resort to trickery of any kind. You can't conceal ignorance; you can only affront the intelligence of others by making them feel you think you can put something over on them.

8. If you are presenting a great deal of data by means of charts and tables, you can keep your audience listening, rather than writing, by announcing that you will make copies of the data available at the end of the meeting.

As with any formula, you must suit it to the occasion. You cannot follow it rigidly. There will always be surprises for you. Your best defense against the unexpected is to prepare well.

Summary

Just as there is a direct relationship to successful companies and the ability to communicate, so there is the same direct relationship between individual success and the ability to skillfully participate in the business meeting. It provides the opportunity to sharpen your knowledge and skills, to learn from others so that you are more valuable to yourself and your company and to expose your talents to your superiors.

Here are some guidelines to help you participate more skillfully:

1. Remember that you are a vital part of a team trying to reach a common objective or you wouldn't have been invited.

2. You will be more valuable to yourself and your company if you keep up with larger management strategy. Read company publications, keep yourself posted on overall company developments. Acquire the habit of problem analysis.

3. Be prepared in depth, both as to your own participation and related aspects of the subject matter.

4. Make an outline of your presentation and rehearse it before time.

5. Use visuals wherever possible to improve your communication.

6. Be open to other points of view.

7. Practice good meeting manners. Don't distract the others.

8. Respect the views of your colleagues. When there are differences of opinion, don't personalize them.

9. Speak up on matters on which you are knowledgeable but do not over-do your participation.

10. Listen actively.

11. Take lots of notes. This is part of active learning. They will be useful in later recall of what transpired.

12. Don't bring up any surprise proposals of which your own boss is not aware, particularly if he is present.

13. Avoid provoking controversy, if at all possible. Try to work out controversies before the meeting.

14. If you don't know your subject, don't try to bluff or resort to trickery.

Notes

Chapter VII

Visual Aids to Clarity

You can build an entire meeting around a few simple, easy-to-make charts or transparencies. You may never have given a presentation before, yet with the help of visual aids and just a little practice you can rank with the experts!

The secret is a simple one. Into your visuals you will have put the very essence of your thinking. Then when you are up before your audience — whether a few people or a roomful — you are not at a loss for words, because you have an outline of thought right before you.

Fundamentally, visual aids are not only essential for effective meeting communication, they are built-in "organizers" for those making a presentation. They force the presenter into pre-planned organization of thought and idea, to concentrate on main points, eliminate secondary or non-essential material, to reduce the complex into one simplified, clearly understandable point. In a sense, a good visual is the good right arm of effective communication.

Some Principles of Visual Communication

You can learn a great deal by listening well to others. In a subsequent chapter, we will go into some pertinent listening techniques because, paradoxically, even people who spend a lot of time in meetings often manage to do a poor job of listening.

It's worse than that. If we first subtract from our investment in communication time the loss due to poor listening and then take another loss because of how little was *retained* of what was heard, it becomes clearly imperative that we find some way of getting a better return from our communication time.

Some General Principles

A chart or a transparency — which is a projection type of chart — should be built around *ideas*, rather than around trick displays. Your visual materials are merely *carrier* devices for presenting ideas more effectively; the ideas are always the starting points. Accordingly, realize first that your visuals can never be better than the thought they present.

Should you start with a sketch or a chart, or should you first work out your entire presentation? The truth probably lies somewhere between. Always remember that you are *selling*. With this in mind, try to identify the main points you want to convey from both your position and the needs and interest of your audience.

For an important presentation of any length you should work out a presentation script. This is a narrative outline or text of what you propose to say. As you develop it, you will have in mind certain visual charts or displays, but it is from this total script that your final needs will be drawn.

Bear in mind that general theories, principles, or rules are not easily absorbed by most people. The tangible is always to be preferred to the abstract or general. Examples are most appreciated when they clarify ideas through reference to practical experiences and problems that the audience members will understand. Your examples must *support* your main ideas. Your examples must not overpower your presentation to the extent that they steal the show or divert attention. As with specific visuals, you should first find your total presentation and then fit in appropriate examples, anecdotes, and humor.

Let's discuss humor briefly. Some situations call for a liberal dosage of light relief. A sales meeting is an example. This is really a dead-serious affair. You are dealing with the very lifeblood of the organization.

There's apt to be a great deal of tension in the air, particularly when the meeting is an all-day or several-day affair. A little humor in good taste can go a long way to relieve audience tension. It can also be used to drive a point home.

But humor has its risks. If you have a mixed audience, don't include any off-color stories! Even though you have an all-male audience, don't tell any bathroom stories. It is not worth risking your entire presentation to tell a story which may offend some and embarrass the rest. When it comes to using members of the audience as characters for your funny stories, be particularly careful. As long as you cast them in a fairly good light, you are on safe ground. As soon as you lean toward making them scapegoats or putting them up for public ridicule, you are on dangerous ground. Your victims may not protest, but they probably won't be amused. The other members of the audience may also side with the victims, whom they will regard as underdogs.

Perhaps a good guideline to follow before the meeting would be to have a *conversation with yourself*, in which you ask these basic questions:

Are my visuals simple, concise, to the point, understandable, believable and authoritative? Are they organized in sequence to reach a logical conclusion? Are they directed to the special interst of those to whom I will be speaking? Do they effectively help me reach my objective? Do I have too many visuals or too few? Would I be convinced if I were in the audience? If you can answer these questions satisfactorily to yourself, you are on your way to an effective presentation.

What to Include

There are three rules which will guide you through the preparation of most visuals. These rules are based on how much the mind can readily grasp and absorb before moving on to the next mental stimulus.

1. One point or relationship per visual;
2. Maximum of 6 or 7 words per line;
3. Maximum of 6 or 7 lines per visual;

The dominance of the single idea must be stressed. You want to concentrate the thought of the entire audience on one theme, one idea, one formula or one key fact before you move ahead. If the audience gets nothing else from a particular visual, you must make it grasp the main point.

If you want your ideas to be understood well, use arguments and examples that build on the familiar. Appeal to the interests and motivations of your individual audience members.

Make up some rough drafts as charts or as visual projections and view them yourself from where the most distant audience member will be seated. If you can't read the smallest print, you will have to use larger letters, even though this means eliminating some material, or going to an additional chart. As a rule, the smallest letters should be about 3 inches high when projected. (Check the section on The Art of a Good Visual for a more detailed explanation.)

Some charts will consist of several lines of reading matter. There is not too much you can do about these except to follow the principles listed above. With a little skill, however, you can sometimes give emphasis to particular words or lines. You will have more flexibility if you combine words, diagrams, pictures, and symbols. Create a center of interest through physical arrangement of the materials and through use of color. If you do not use color, you might vary the heaviness of lines, or in some other way contrast light and dark. Emphasis can also be achieved by the relative size of individual lines and figures.

Simplicity is another rule. If you keep to the one-main-idea rule, you will also tend to achieve simplicity. Every visual should be crisp, dynamic, and pithy, the text tight and bright. Every unnecessary or questionably useful item should be eliminated, even though it's a single word. Generally speaking, use the shorter of two alternate words, although you should use language that puts ideas across. Use bold lines and forms; avoid fine scale. Cartoons and other art work can be powerful adjuncts, but if you go overboard on artistry or color for their own sake you will risk diverting the viewer's focus from the main idea.

Department of Second Thought

Thomas Edison used to tell about writing angry letters and saving them unmailed until he had had a chance to cool off and re-read them. Then, most of the time he would tear the letters up.

This story underscores the need for giving yourself enough time in developing your presentation to allow your ideas to become a little seasoned. You will also have more opportunity to get other people's ideas. Although you may not always have as much time as you would like, particularly when someone has given you a short-notice assignment, here is one sequence you should follow:

1. Do a thorough job of research, filing materials, other references, and suggestions of colleagues and experts.

2. Prepare a rough outline which may or may not include your first ideas for visual displays.

3. Make a list of the key ideas in your presentation as developed in the outline or written draft.

4. Develop your visuals in semi-final form around these key ideas, bringing in supplementary examples and anecdotes.

5. Try your presentation on one or more other people. Keep an open mind. Be willing to revise, *revise*, and REVISE.

If time permits, let a day intervene between each of the important steps, but at least try to get an independent reaction to your tentative presentation.

Techniques That Emphasize the Man

There are some techniques of presentation in which you need have little to do. You can put slides into a machine, press button, and then lean back to think about what you're going to have for dinner. A record or tape will carry your voice and, through intermittent beeps, opearte a slide projector automatically. There are two things wrong with this method. One is that it is not ideally suited for short-notice meetings. The other is that it is too "canned" — the audience will feel that the speaker himself has nothing to say.

Slide presentations have their good points, and we'll go into them below, but here we will discuss those methods of presentation which emphasize the personal message of the speaker. These include the use of the blackboard, easel pads, flannelboards, charts, and overhead projectors. We were exposed to some or all of them when we started school; the overhead projector is a little more modern, although it has been on the market for over twenty years. As it has become easier to make projection transparencies this has become the most flexible and undoubtedly the most effective and broadly useful of the tools of visual communication.

Fundamentally, blackboards, easels, and flannelboards are highly restricted methods of visual communication. They have all been around for a long time. They are all relatively inexpensive, but what is gained in terms of inexpensiveness in the use of these methods is sacrificed in one degree or other by lack of flexibility, quality, low degree of visual impact and unprofessionalism.

We live in an age attuned to television in which audiences are accustomed to professionally produced visual presentations. Any visual presentation today which does not take advantage of available modern visual vehicles is likely to attract negative responses if for no other reason than guilt-by-association with obsolete or restricted visual mehtods of communication.

However, we will examine these methods of visual presentation briefly.

The Blackboard

The blackboard is perhaps one of the oldest methods of visual communication next to *graffiti*, written on walls, which dates to antiquity. It has the advantages of simplicity, low cost and spontaneity. All that is needed is a chalk with which to write an idea on the board as soon as it occurs, and an eraser to erase it. However, it should be used only before small groups. Before a large audience the chalk line loses visibility. Also, the speaker runs the risk of losing control over his audience when he turns his back to write. Squeaking or broken chalk and dropped erasers can prove to be a distraction and embarrassment to both speaker and audience. In fact, in this day and age one should regard this method of communication as being inadequate for most business meeting situations.

Easel Pad Presentations

The easel pad essentially is an over-sized scratch pad mounted on a firm surface attached to an easel. It's effective use is pretty much confined to small groups. The speaker writes on the pad with black or colored grease pencils, colored chalks or felt-tipped marking pens.

It offers some flexibility in that the pages can be flipped back and forth at will or hung on walls. It also invokes a sense of spontaneous presentation.

Flannelboards

Anyone who has seen an old time movie lampooning business hucksterism probably has seen a flannelboard or, as it is sometimes called, a slapboard or stickboard. It consists of a piece of flannel stretched on a firm surface onto which one can "slap" simple written captions or other materials. It is well suited to sales meetings and other situations of persuasion when a flair for showmanship is called for. However, its use may have a negative effect on today's sophisticated audiences.

Opaque Projection

The opaque projector may also be included in the group of visual aids with restricted utility. It is a professional version of the old-fashioned magic lantern. Any written or printed matter, black-and-white or color, is illuminated quite well and its image reflected from a mirror through a lens and then onto a screen. It can also project images of flat physical objects, such as coins and small machine parts. Theoretically, the opaque projector is a great convenience because printed matter of any kind can be projected right on the spot. However, because of several disadvantages, most projectors are left to gather dust in the supply cupboard. In the first place, they are large and bulky. They get very hot, necessitating noisy built-in blowers. They must be used in a darkened room, so the speaker is at a disadvantage, no matter where he stands. For practical purposes, we can forget about the opaque projector in the business meeting.

Chart Presentations

The prepared chart is one of the most common mediums of business communication. From the speaker's standpoint he has his presentation all made up without the necessity to have any special notes. Although it may take a little while to have charts prepared, it takes much less time than preparing slides or filmstrips, both of which will be discussed below.

For most purposes, elaborate charts are not needed either. There is a technique of preparing "rough finals," which cuts costs and may be more effective because of the feeling of spontaneity. More elaborately designed charts may be justified when you are making very important presentations which also may be reproduced for additional corporate use.

However, the old method of chart presentation should give way to the new system of presenting them as overhead projection transparencies or, as they are called, electric flip-charts. Any chart lends itself well to overhead projection, commands greater audience control, visibility and flexibility. These advantages will be discussed in the following section.

Overhead Projection

Whatever you can do with any of the media already described, you can do more effectively with an overhead projector. This is the type of projector that has gained widespread acceptance as a classroom teaching aid on all levels of education.

A transparency is simply placed on the stage of the projector and the image is then reflected at a 90° angle onto a dull-finish screen mounted on a wall or stand.

Although most other projectors must be placed in the middle or at the rear of the audience, the overhead projector is right up front with the speaker, who can face his audience with the machine by his side.

Other important advantages of this technique are:

1. Presentations can be given in a fully lighted room.

2. The overhead projector can be easily turned on and off at the flick of a switch, permitting the speaker to direct the attention of the audience from the screen to himself and back again at will.

3. Because of its unique projection qualities, the overhead projector makes every seat in the meeting room a vantage point.

4. Material can be revealed point by point so that attention is fixed and participants cannot read ahead or jump to conclusions, a technique known as "revelation."

5. Because of its simplicity of construction, the use of an overhead projector poses little likelihood of a mechanical failure which could ruin a presentation. There is a greater possibility of mechanical failure or mal-operation with more complicated equipment such as slide, filmstrip, motion picture or video tape recording equipment.

6. Does not require expensive and time-consuming technical processing that is involved in slides, filmstrips and movies.

7. Does not distract the presentation with rustle of paper, clacking or chalk squeaks such as is present in the use of easel boards, flannelboards or blackboards. There is also no distracting noise emitted by the overhead projector as there is with film equipment.

8. You do not need a special technician to operate overhead equipment.

The single factor that is bringing projectors into more common usage as probably the most effective tool of communication for daily internal meetings, as well as for more formal presentations, is the facility with which transparencies can be made quickly and inexpensively. Virtually any document, illustration or diagram can be converted into a transparency for immediate projection in a matter of seconds. The original document, along with a sheet of transparency film, is passed through an office copying machine, producing a ready-to-project transparency. This development eliminates the use of chemicals, photography and other costly reproduction processes.

The transparency itself becomes a unique method of communication that offers the following features:

1. The meeting leader can write on a blank sheet of transparency film with a grease pencil or felt-tip marking pen.

2. He can project sales forecasts, complex financial data, engineering drawings and other elaborate material without the necessity of preparing special artwork.

3. He can underline, circle or make notations directly on the transparency while it is being projected, to emphasize certain key points.

4. Color transparencies, positives and negatives, can be used to keep the presentation moving along.

5. Overlays of succeeding sheets of film which add information to the original transparency have many uses including comparative sales curves.

6. Pieces of colored sheet plastic can be added to black-and-white transparencies; for example, to dramatize a bar graph.

Another major advantage of the overhead projection technique is the chance it gives you to turn the preparation of your visuals over to your secretary.

Once she has mastered the few simple techniques of making good overhead projection transparencies, the visuals for your next presentation can be put together quickly and inexpensively. The complicated visual that would have cost you many dollars can now be made for pennies. Sources of visual communications materials can also be sources of training for businessmen and their secretaries in these techniques.

Slides

Projection presentations based on the use of 35 mm slides have been very popular. Such slides are made in standard 2″ × 2″mounts, using 35mm film. Theoretically this format enables you to do a certain amount of home-grown photography, but the typical slide presentation usually has to be worked up in the company art department.

Because the equipment is small and portable a slide presentation can be taken almost anywhere. Slides are much more flexible than filmstrips in that their sequence can be changed and, thus, combinations made to suit the occasion. You can keep a whole library of slides from which you make a selection.

Slides are suitable for multiple remote presentations, but they are expensive. You can send a set of slides to a couple of hundred different branches and be assured that the message will be conveyed in identical manner. You need not worry that somebody in Butte, Montana, is going to make a change or a mistake. You can even send along a pre-recorded magnetic tape synchronized with the slide sequence. The sound on the tape activates the slide changer at just the right moment.

A picture and sound presentation can be even more conveniently prepared with a projector we manufacture: The Sound-on-Slide System.

This is a self-contained projector-recorder that uses trays of special slide frames, each bearing a 35 mm slide surrounded by a magnetic audio disc. Because the picture and its sound track form a separate entity, you are not faced with the problem of synchronizing sight and sound, nor with the laborious task of trying to edit a continuous strip of magnetic recording tape.

With slides, you can turn out excellent presentations by using relatively untrained meeting leaders. Hence, it is an excellent medium for people who only occasionally are called upon to make presentations.

There is also a dark side to using slides. For best effect, they must be used in a darkened room, which presents the discussion leader with some unique problems. He must fight against an audience whose attention he may be unable to hold under cover of darkness. He must also fight an uphill battle to be an effective leader — especially when his slides are so superior they tend to steal the show. The listener is also faced with a problem of taking notes in the same darkness that confounds the meeting leader.

Following are some suggestions for making a slide presentation:

1. Edit the slides beforehand to make sure you have the right ones and that they are all in proper sequence, with none upside down or wrong way around.

2. Limit the number of slides to the time available. Usually, you can figure on 15 to 20 seconds for each slide; some will take less.

3. Rehearse the entire presentation. Make any changes or notes beforehand. Make sure the slides are clean, since a big fingerprint or big black specks cannot fail to deglamorize your presentation.

4. Set up a lighted lectern so that you can read your notes as you make your presentation.

5. Use a remote control projector or an assistant to change the slides so that you will be able to face the audience as much as possible.

6. Tell the audience a little of your total presentation before you get started. Then lead somewhat into each new slide before you flash it. In this way, you prepare the audience for what is coming and make it a little more intense.

7. Never show slides after lunch, because you will come into competition with the effects of a full stomach working in a darkened room! The best time for slides is right after the coffee break.

Filmstrips

Filmstrip projectors have about the same advantages and disadvantages as slide projectors with one big difference: because the films run in a strip, they cannot be changed in sequence. The disadvantage is loss of flexibility, which becomes a plus when you have to send a few hundred presentations out around the country at least expense. You can be sure that each presentation will go off as planned at the home office, with no slides dropping out of sequence.

Motion Pictures

Movies are controversial in business presentations. Maybe it is because they suggest entertainment by their very nature. Their pros and cons have been argued over the years. In an issue of *Sales Meetings Magazine*, two articles argued the point. The first was "I Like Movies," and the second "I Hate Movies." Why two such opposing opinions?

The first author suggested that "motion pictures are the nearest thing to real experience. They communicate ideas with greater penetration. Movies are the modern medium." His opponent countered that "movies are expensive, ineffective, wasteful and overrated. Why pay for motion? How many times do you need it? Not very often!"

The truth is distributed between both viewpoints. Movies are here to stay as an excellent audio-visual aid combining sight, sound, color and motion to give the audience a realistic experience with high retention. We use them for explaining processes, operations and concepts that call for a continuous sequence. An example would be training films in which people and objects are active. Another is the "tour" of assembly lines to see machines and people in action.

Motion pictures are limited for everyday use, as becomes brutally apparent when you look at the cost: about $1,000 a minute for an action sequence that is pretty well locked in place. A few years ago we made a movie to demonstrate some office equipment machines. It cost us a great deal of money. Six months after its production the movie was obsolete because of changes in two of the machines.

Although the initial cost is high, if you are going to make a great number of prints, the motion picture may still be the preferred medium. 3M sent training films on the use of overhead projectors to 500 schools across the country. When you divide that number of films into the original cost, $1,000 a minute drops down to $2.00 a minute per film. And when you consider that each film has several showings, the unit cost per showing goes down even more.

For discussion meetings, the motion picture is not out of the question, but you must remember that it does not permit discussion feedback during the actual showing. The lecturer should run the film beforehand in order to be thoroughly familiar with its contents.

Video Tape Recording

The impact of video tape use in the business arena is growing rapidly. While it is not expected to replace other audio-visual systems, but rather complement them because of its unique capabilities, its use will continue to grow as technology is improved and costs reduced.

Video tape recordings in business offer advantages similar to motion picture film — integration of theme, sight, sound, color and motion. At the same time, this medium offers additional advantages not now possible with motion pictures. It does not require costly processing as film does. The tape can be erased and used over again indefinitely.

Copies of the tape can be dubbed to other tapes or transferred to film if large distribution is required. The video tape playback permits immediate re-running of a sequence and changes can easily be made in a presentation. Sections can be deleted or added quickly with no processing cost. Thus, the meeting leader can rehearse his presentation and immediately review the tape in order to judge his effectiveness and make changes. Video tape presentations can also be transmitted to any number of locations by micro-wave or coaxial cable. A basic system, consisting of a camera, recorder and monitors, can be installed quickly and easily; the operating cost is relatively low.

However, such special advantages carry with them a high price tag. The costs could range from hundreds to several thousands of dollars, depending on how sophisticated a system is required. In addition, operation of VTR equipment requires a moderate degree of technical know-how and a small staff to produce the presentations.

Room Layout Guidelines

There are a few simple guidelines for the proper placement of screens and projectors, room orientation and screen sizes, which, when followed, add up to an effective presentation. These guidelines are listed below, with accompanying diagrams and some tables showing proper screen sizes:

1. The screens must be placed in the corner of the room to allow clear viewing by all the audience. The instructor and projector otherwise will obstruct the view of the screen.

2. The screen is placed in the corner to the right of the speaker

Screen Size

Screen size must be equated to distance between screen and person sitting furthest from the screen. Screen size dictates magnification possible from projector to screen.

Furthest Distance to Screen	20'	25'	30'	35'	40'	45	50'
Screen Size	50"x50"	60"x60"	70"x70"	84"x84" (7'x7')	96"x96" (8'x8')	9'x9'	10'x10'

This information is based upon 3M Visual Products' template for minimum image size, stock number 78-1751-0764-4.

Room Size vs. Ceiling Height

Distance From Front to Rear	0 – 30	30 – 40	40 – 50	50 – 60	Over 60
Ceiling Height	9	10	11	12	Over 12

Projector to Screen Distances

Standard overhead projectors such as those sold by 3M Company are manufactured with a 14-inch focal length projection lens.

Projector to screen distance depends upon screen size; the larger the screen, the greater distance required.

For 14-Inch Focal Length Projectors

Projector to Screen Distance	84" (7')	98" (8' 2")	112" (9' 4")	131" (10' 11")	148" (12' 4")	165" (13' 9")	182" (15' 2")
Screen Size	50"x50"	60"x60"	70"x70"	84"x84"	96"x96"	9'x9'	10'x10'

For Model 88 Desktop Projector, 10.5-Inch Focal Length

Projector to Screen Distance	63"	73"	84"	99"	111"
Screen Size	50" x 50"	60" x 60"	70" x 70"	84" x 84"	96" x 96"

Screen Size vs. Projector Distance for Filmstrip, 35 mm Slide Projectors or 3M Sound-on-Slide System

Projector to Screen Distance	13'	16'	19'	22'	25'
Screen Size	40" x 40"	50" x 50"	60" x 60"	70" x 70"	80" x 80"

as he faces the audience (for right-handed speakers). This allows the speaker to write on the stage of the projector while facing the audience, thus maintaining close contact with the audience.

3. Matte finish screens must be used because of the sharp angles at which the audience must view the screen. Our tests have shown that the audience will have no problem viewing images from matte finish screens at angles down to 25 degrees. Beaded or lenticular screens will not work at these sharp angles.

4. Permanent screens can be mounted on either the ceiling or a wall but should be mounted far enough away from the wall to allow anti-keystoning tilt. New ceiling mounts which allow more complete flexibility are now available.

5. Projection screens should not cover an entrance if permanently mounted in a room.

6. To save space, the speaker should be located at one end of the room's narrow dimension.

7. The proper size of the projection screen depends on the size of the room and distance between persons seated farthest from the screen and the screen itself. The screen size table on page 55 indicates proper screen size requirements. The additional charts show projector to screen size variations with different size screens.

8. The screens must be tilted forward at the top (or back at the bottom) to prevent image keystoning. The amount of tilt is determined by assuming the top of the screen to be a certain height above floor level and the projector head to be 58 inches above floor level. As an example, a 60 × 60 inch screen requires 13 inches of forward tilt under these circumstances when ceiling height is nine feet. The top of the screen must be the same distance from the projector lens as the bottom of the lens in order to avoid keystoning.

9. Overhead lights directly over the projection screen should be avoided or should be controlled by a separate switch.

10. Overhead projectors, slide projectors, film strip projectors and movie projectors can be used in the rooms described. Locate the slide and filmstrip projectors about twice the distance from the screen as the overhead and temporarily remove the overhead projector so it does not block the projected image. Movie projectors can be used from the rear of the room by changing the screen angle slightly.

11. Avoid very large rooms that have low ceilings. As distances between audience and screen increase the projection screen size must increase. Low ceilings limit screen size and therefore projector usefulness. As a rule of thumb, the *minimum* ceiling height should be 12-15 feet.

The diagrams on these pages depict graphically good and bad screen arrangements. Use in conjunction with tables on page 95, they will aid you in choosing the proper room and screen.

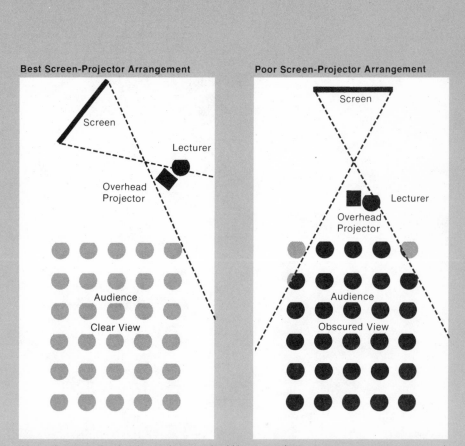

Best Screen-Projector Arrangement

Screen

Lecturer

Overhead Projector

Audience

Clear View

Poor Screen-Projector Arrangement

Screen

Overhead Projector

Lecturer

Audience

Obscured View

When using an overhead projector, the room should be arranged so that the view of the audience to the screen is not blocked by the speaker and the projector.

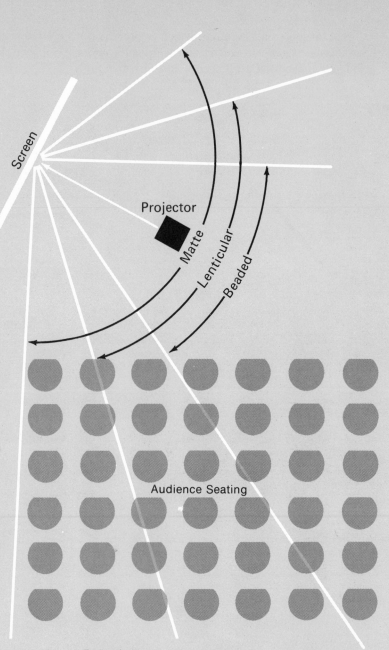

Screen

Projector

Matte
Lenticular
Beaded

Audience Seating

Maximum Image Reflection
Angles shown indicate direction of maximum image reflection from different types of screens.

Portion of the audience sitting beyond the angles shown for a particular screen see only a faint unclear image on the screen.

Notes

Notes

How to Make a Technical Presentation

When I think of the subject of specialists making presentations I am reminded of the rather ancient anecdote of the politician who was delivering a lengthy oration in a small midwestern town. One of his assistants arrived late, and as he ran up the steps to the meeting place he met one of the townsfolk coming down. Ever analytical about how his boss was doing, the assistant inquired, "Is Senator Anderson speaking in there?"

"Yep," answered the local.

"What is he talking about?" asked the assistant.

The old fellow adjusted a piece of straw from one corner of his mouth to the other and replied matter of factly, "He didn't say."

How many times a day, a week, a month or a year do business meetings end with the audience ready to give a similar reply? The number of valuable hours lost in business meetings where no real communication occurs can never be calculated, but it must be enormous. I would guess that it is the greatest loss suffered in the business world today. And most of it a loss that is needless.

There perhaps is no single factor which impedes effective communication more than the use of language not understandable to an audience. If one is making a presentation to a specialized audience which understands the specialized terms, fine. But more often than not, that will not be the case. A technical presentation will be necessary to convince those in the fields of finance, sales, production, etc., of the value of the proposal under discussion.

As we have noted in the appendix on **THE ART OF A GOOD VISUAL**, we all use "in-group" words, phrases and expressions in our particular life occupations that are foreign or fuzzy in meaning to others. The insistence upon using specialized terms when addressing those on the "outside" can be attributed to various factors — habit, an ego force designed to impress others with the importance or complexity of one's job, even a witting or unwitting motive to obscure.

Whatever the underlying reason, it is a high price to pay for bad communication. It is unlikely to impress anyone. No one places much value on confusion. And most certainly a businessman who is always pressed for time is not going to appreciate a waste of that time listening to a presentation from which he has learned nothing of value except that the presenter is a very bad communicator who might just as well have spoken in Mandarin Chinese.

Not long ago, the president of one of the largest corporations in the country called his controller and asked, "I hear a lot of talk around here by our computer people about the need for a Management Information System. What is a management information system?"

The controller replied, "Well, a P and L statement is a good example. It's an information system to tell you what's happening."

The president replied, with some exasperation. "Well, why the hell didn't they say that? I think what we need first of all is a crash course on effective communication for our computer people so we can decipher the information we do get."

The moral is: Unless you are talking to one of your own group, leave your specialized, in-group language behind. If you cannot, at least define the meaning of that language.

In a sense, the specialist making a presentation is at a disadvantage because, more than likely, he has not been attuned to the world of selling. But we are all salesmen, regardless of our occupations, in that we are called upon from time to time to convince others of the validity of our ideas or the correctness of our propositions.

There is the anecdote of the management consultant who went to the police station to pay a parking fine.

"Management consultant," he said, when the policeman asked for his occupation. "Management consultant?" was the quizzical response by the desk officer, who was contemplating the half-inch into which he had to fit those two long words. After only a moment's hesitation, the policeman wrote: "Salesman."

The moral of this story reaches into almost every aspect of life. In some sense, each of us must sell his way at every turn. A business meeting, whether it persuades directly or reaches a decision, also involves you in the selling of ideas. To a very great extent, the rewards of life go out to those who do the best selling job. You can build the best mousetrap possible, but people won't necessarily beat their paths to your door. They expect you to come to them with a convincing story.

If you are a professional man — an engineer, scientist, economist, controller, statistician, biologist, mathematician, computer programmer or other technician — you are part of a growing band of people who are reshaping the world. You are becoming a part of a powerful force in the conduct of business and industrial enterprise. You are one of the new communicators. You have the message that people are waiting to hear. You are a part of the scientific and technological wave which has created entirely new industries and reshaped or outdated old ones. You are in the vanguard of dramatic new things to come.

Your Achilles heel, if you have one, is that you haven't learned how to communicate well. The exceptions are in the minority. The reason is a simple one. You spend so many years in school concentrating on the subject matter of your profession, you simply cannot devote very much time to the processes of communication. Furthermore, the idea of having to sell someone your ideas may be reprehensible to you. Your task is to design the better mousetrap; maybe even to build it. "Someone else" will have to sell it.

This may be true if you are content to confine yourself to the laboratory or the drafting board. But in order to step across the threshold of management — to become a project manager, or a general manager — you must assume responsibilities for communication . . . and for selling. If you pick up almost any professional or trade journal, you will find this universal lament: professional people need to learn how to communicate more effectively. Recently, the Western Electronic Conference (WESCON), having faced the technical-speaker problem many times before, published a booklet it sent out in advance of its annual convention. The booklet was entitled "Techniques for Better Talks at WESCON (and instructions for session chairmen)."

Making a technical presentation so that it doesn't sound like one is really easier than you might think. It calls for a little advance preparation and some rehearsals, which make good sense in any event. What can really turn you into a seemingly professional speaker or presentation expert is a clever use of a few visuals.

Visual Impact

The steps you take in planning your presentation should include careful selection of the appropriate communications tools. What an audience retains depends a great deal on how the information is presented. And since there is abundant evidence supporting the fact that our eyes play a primary role in this regard, visual aids should be part of your presentation.

The most commonly used tools of visual presentation are cardboard display charts, transparencies for overhead projectors, 35mm slides, pad displays, and chalkboard presentations. As explained earlier, each of these has its advantages and disadvantages. At the 3M Company we prefer the overhead projector, because we think it offers the greatest flexibility and visual impact for most meeting and conference situations. We use other media and techniques, whenever they are most appropriate.

Visual aids offer a hidden advantage which the audience cannot see, but which it can feel. They force the speaker to organize his thinking. They cause the speaker to bring elements of the discussion into common relationship. Obviously, the more the speaker does to clarify his thinking, the more likely he is to communicate this to his listeners.

Visual aids channel the thinking of the audience members. They do so, that is, if they are well conceived and if the speaker leads his audience logically through the presentation, one step at a time. Another advantage of visual aids is that they summarize the key points in a discussion and emphasize those that are most important.

Visual aids also are extremely useful in presenting technical data and concepts. This is particularly true if, as is often the case, the presentation is being made to sales or merchandising personnel whose technical orientation and vocabularies may be limited but who, nonetheless, must understand the product in order to sell it effectively.

A good example of this sort of approach is the following description of a Fresnel lens, used in conjunction with a simplified transparency. The description alone is this:

"A Fresnel lens is a condenser lens with a discontinuous incremental surface where the slope of each increment corresponds to the slope of a continuous curve or usually the refractive surface of a lens.

"It does the job of a solid glass lens but weighs less, occupies less volume and generally is less expensive.

"The configuration of a Fresnel lens is best understood by considering a conventional glass condenser lens in cross section. If now this lens is considered in segments and the actual refracting surfaces are considered in minimum thicknesses, we have the elements of a Fresnel lens. Thin plastic sections corresponding to these minimum thicknesses will perform essentially the same function as the thick glass lens.

"In actual production the plastic sections take an angled shape, with the angled surfaces tangent to the curved reflecting surfaces of the glass lens."

This description, if presented only verbally, undoubtedly would leave a good many salesmen hanging on the ropes. Keyed to the transparency reproduced here, (Illustration a), each step in the description suddenly becomes clear, even to the uninitiated.

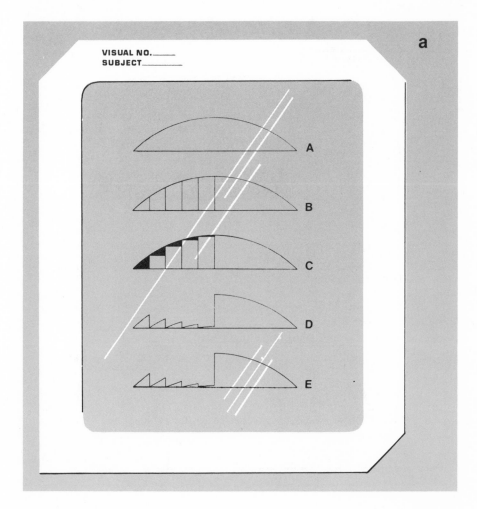

Here is another technical description simplified through the use of a transparency and an overhead projector:

"Today I want to discuss some of the characteristics of screws. You can well imagine that if I passed a screw out to everyone in the room I would have a difficult time holding your attention to specific points of interest, besides causing a great deal of confusion and distraction.

"In contrast, let's use this illustration on the overhead projector (Illustration b). A screw is a device with a cylindrical shank from which projects a continuous helical rib or thread. The size of the thread may vary and it is therefore necessary to design its characteris-

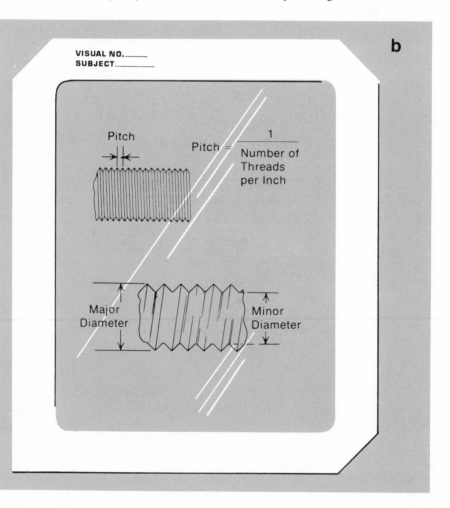

tics. This is done by counting the number of complete revolutions the thread makes per inch. By the use of our transparency scale, we see that in this case we have six threads in one inch.

"The reciprocal of the number of threads per inch is defined as the pitch (Indicate equation on transparency). In this case, we have a pitch of 1/6 or .167 inches per thread.

"Referring now to the second portion of this visual, we see that in addition to the pitch we must define the size of thread on the cylindrical shank. This is done by referring to the bottom portion of each thread as the minor diameter and the peak of each thread as the major diameter.

"We now have covered most of the fundamental characteristics of screws without confusion. And by removing the visual from the screen (turn off the projector) we can continue along our line of discussion without distraction."

Here is a third technical description making use of a simplified transparency:

"The mechanics of overhead projectors are difficult to illustrate. I would hate to take the time to recreate on a blackboard the construction of an overhead projector due to its complexity. It would take too much time to hand out literature to each and every person; not to mention that you would probably be lost during my discussion. I certainly would not take the time to dismantle one.

"The easiest approach is to make a transparency showing the optical arrangement of the projector and place it on the stage of the overhead (Illustration c). Before you now you see the basic optical layout of a majority of overhead projectors. The components that are included in the optical system can be followed through in this manner:

"First we have a lamp. The lamp produces a beam of light one half of which passes directly through the optical system to the right, the other half of which is collected by the reflector. The reflector returns the light to the lamp and thus allows this light to continue through the optical system to the right.

"Following the lamp a heat filter is introduced to remove the unwanted radiation. At this point, however, the light is still diverging and must be brought to a narrower cone of light with a simple condensing lens.

"The next optical element is a mirror which renders the optical path vertical and, since it is not involved in the image making process, we may use a more durable mirror, called a rear surface mirror.

"Above this mirror is the heart of the projector — the Fresnel condenser lens. This thin, flat extremely efficient element not only collects

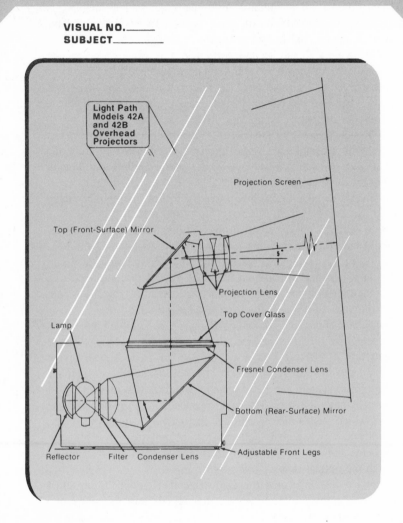

VISUAL NO._____
SUBJECT_____

Light Path
Models 42A
and 42B
Overhead
Projectors

Projection Screen

Top (Front-Surface) Mirror

5°

Projection Lens

Lamp

Top Cover Glass

Fresnel Condenser Lens

Bottom (Rear-Surface) Mirror

Adjustable Front Legs

Reflector   Filter   Condenser Lens

the light coming from the lamp but changes this diverging beam of light into a converging beam of light above the stage.

"To protect the Fresnel lens, we have a top cover glass which serves as a writing surface as well as a protector. The light then continues to the head and is intercepted by the top front surface mirror. The mirror in this case is involved in the image making process and, therefore, the best optical surface must be used, hence a front surface mirror.

"This mirror serves not only in reducing the height of the projector but turns the optical path toward the viewing screen, or projection screen. In addition, the mirror inverts the image on the screen, so that it will be upright for the audience. All this light then passes through the projection lens and it is the projection lens that deciphers the image out of this condensing path and forms the image on the screen of whatever is laid on the cover glass.

"We have just covered most of the basic elements required in an overhead projector, described their utility and have indicated some of the various designs that are possible. Any approach without the use of this visual aid would have taken hours to cover the same amount."

In another area, a useful and interesting visual technique has been developed at 3M for converting parts cost figures to the eventual retail offering price of a product. The technique is essentially a series of related nomographs plotted in three quadrants and reproduced as an overhead projector transparency for use in meetings.

This calculation is generally somewhat involved, and the explanation of the procedure can easily lead to confusion if not done carefully. Our experience has been that the process is more effectively communicated with the use of visual aids. But an example would serve to illustrate this idea more clearly.

You would first project quadrant A (Figure 1) which shows the parts cost, X axis, plotted against the total factory cost, which may vary depending on the complexity of the machine under consideration. To make the conversion, a complexity ratio line (parts cost/total factory cost) is plotted. The more labor and control checking necessary to produce a machine, the lower the value of the complexity ratio and the steeper the plotted curve. This on transfer to the Y axis shows a resulting higher factory cost.

Quadrant A is represented here with two examples plotted simultaneously. The simpler unit, A, with a complexity ratio of .85 shows a hypothetical parts cost of $90.00. The total factory cost is shown on the Y axis at approximately $105.00. The difference, $15.00, is

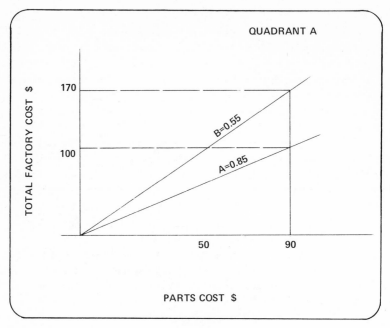

Figure 1

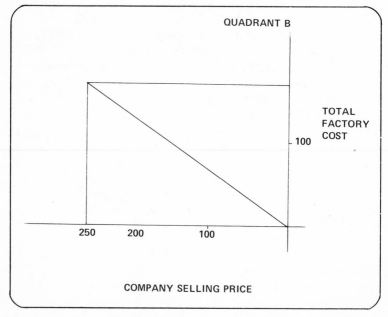

Figure 2

dedicated to labor and checking. On the other hand, with the same parts cost of $90.00, unit B — with a complexity ratio of .55 — shows a total factory cost of $170.00, allocating almost $80.00 for labor and inspection.

Converting the factory cost thus obtained to the selling price is accomplished in quadrant B (Figure 2). The slope of the diagonal line is a function of the mark up necessary to produce profit. In this example, the unit costing $170.00 may be sold by the company to its dealers for $250.00. This value is obtained by reading the X axis value directly below the intersection of the diagonal and the $170.00 Y axis value line.

Now, following a procedure established in quadrants A and B, we use quadrant C to convert the dealer price to an estimated retail price (Figure 3). This, of course, is an estimate based on the dealer's particular circumstances of business. In this case, the retail price would amount to approximately $420.00. Combining the three quadrants on a single overhead transparency (Figure 4) permits rapid comparisons of the effect of changes in parts costs and selling price or the influence of simplifying assembly on selling costs. The decision making process is thereby speeded up and made clearer for all involved.

The overhead transparency has also proven useful as a medium for artists' renditions of various new product components. This method eliminates the great expense of having the artist prepare large three-dimensional drawings on hardboard. The smaller size of the transparency (8½″ × 10½″) provides a more comfortable — and far less expensive — medium for the artist. In addition, having a model illustrated on a transparency rather than a large chart permits a greater degree of security for a company.

Summary

We emphasize that visual aids be conceived and prepared after you have first developed the total strategy of your presentation. Then you can determine where they can be most usefully introduced and where you should rely on oral discussion.

The following are some of the main uses of visual aids:
1. To open a discussion with an arresting display

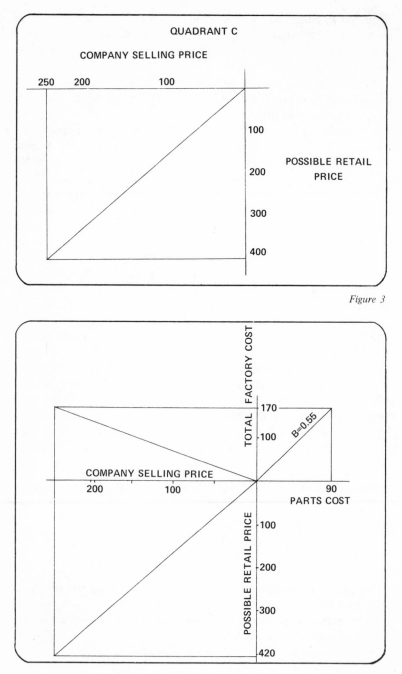

QUADRANT C

COMPANY SELLING PRICE

250   200   100

100

POSSIBLE RETAIL
PRICE

200

300

400

Figure 3

TOTAL FACTORY COST

170

100   B=0.55

COMPANY SELLING PRICE

200   100

90

PARTS COST

100

POSSIBLE RETAIL PRICE

200

300

420

Figure 4

2. To channel thinking
3. To emphasize key points
4. To present financial or statistical data in understandable ways
5. To show comparisons
6. To show relationships
7. To show complex processes in visual form
8. To explain new concepts with the aid of pictures and diagrams

Notes

Chapter IX

Communicating Financial Information

Perhaps each of us regards his particular job as more important than another's. Certainly each job has its degree of importance or there would be no reason for its existence. However, one business position has not always been awarded its just importance and that is the fellow who communicates to management the information on whether the company ship is proceeding on an orderly and profitable course or whether it is floundering, or likely to flounder, on a very red and rocky P and L statement.

Perhaps it is because financial people, as with others in technical areas, have acquired the language barrier affliction — using "in-group" language not readily understandable to others — not being able to get to the point — to communicate.

There is an old joke attributed to people in various technical areas which relates, "Don't ask Henry for the time. He'll give you a detailed lecture on how a watch is made, but you'll never find out what time it is."

If the purpose of a business enterprise is to realize a just profit for services or goods rendered then the most vital information necessary to achievement of that goal is to know at all times the answer to the question: "What is our profit in relation to our costs?"

That vital information is supplied by the company's financial people. It is they who read the sales-cost barometer and send out the signals, good or bad.

When speaking before a group of financial people not long ago, the chairman of the board of one of the largest U.S. corporations likened the respective roles of the controller and the manager in business to the specialist in the medical world who diagnoses the ailment and the surgeon who operates on that ailment.

The controller is the diagnostician who determines where the company is ill and the manager is the surgeon who determines how to correct the illness. Obviously the manager-surgeon could also be the diagnostician but it would leave him just that much less time to get at the business of solving the problems.

That is why, said the board chairman, it is so important for the financial man to communicate his information accurately, quickly and simply.

It is not an impossible task. Many of the guidelines for effective communication are contained in the Appendix, The Art of a Good Visual. But we will offer a specific example for financial people in the following pages.

When Dun's Review asked 300 top executives to nominate the 10 best-managed companies in U.S. industry, 3M Company was chosen as one of them. Dun's Review also asked the 300 executives who make up its Presidents' Panel what is the most outstanding ability of each of the 10 companies nominated by the members of the Panel. From the replies, the six most common rules of good management were selected. Two of these are particularly pertinent to this book. They are:

A proficient communications system, a particularly tricky device that vast segments of industry have yet to master.

An active training program that keeps new managers continually pressing to the fore and established managers on their toes.

Our company uses meetings to communicate and we also use them for the development of new managers. Very high in this scheme of things comes our financial presentation meeting.

The annual review is a standard practice throughout industry. It can serve as a dynamic tool of planning, or it can be a dull and disheartening duty. 3M has had an annual review for many, many years. For a long time, it was not an exciting experience. As the company grew, the preparation time, the cost of charts and other materials, and the presentation time grew to very sizable proportions. There was even talk of discontinuing the review. Then something happened to change the whole picture: the advent of the overhead projector!

Before we switched from charts and other visual devices to the use of transparencies, our presentation costs for the annual reviews had been approximately $100,000. Through the use of the transparencies, some simplified techniques of presentation, and the elimination of expensive art work, our costs dropped to $5,000. Perhaps even more important, we cut a great deal of the time that heretofore had gone into preparation and presentation — time that now can be used for other business activities.

The speed of transparency making overcomes one of the great bugaboos of corporate life — the need to maintain security on private corporate information. This also is pertinent in certain government work performed by industry. Without any technical knowledge or skill, the speaker can make a transparency right in the room for immediate display. When the meeting is over, he can destroy it, or put it in his pocket or briefcase.

This is a general chapter on the presentation of financial information. The techniques to be described can be used with or without the overhead projector.

What Management Needs to Know

There has been a quiet revolution taking place in the world of industrial finance. While top management is as much concerned as ever with accounting for its financial resources, it now sees the accountant's job as something more than tabulating the balance sheet and the profit and loss statement. The company wants information that will tell whether it is making a profit today and whether it is likely to make a profit tomorrow in each of the important aspects of the business.

The pattern of financial reporting, up to the corporate level, is much the same at 3M as at many other corporations.

The Pyramid of Reporting

Each of the 31 divisions and subsidiaries of 3M has a monthly management committee meeting, made up of the division vice president, the production manager, the technical director, the sales manager, the division engineer, and the controller. This committee reviews the division's operations and reports on them to the corporate management. The routine way of doing this is through distribution of minutes, which enable corporate management to keep abreast of current developments throughout the company.

Until our new look in financial reporting, this topic used to be the last thing on the agenda. Everyone in the room hoped against hope that time would run out before the financial report could be presented. It included a great amount of detail through which we laboriously led the members of the committee. The members were brave and they were polite, but they suffered. Ironically, because there was so much information to give them, very little actually got through.

Under the present system, to use the Duplicating Products Division as an example, the nature of the financial presentation is different each month. Moreover, it is now usually presented at the beginning of the meeting to set its tone. That is quite a change. As an example, for the month of January, the divisional controller would compare that month's operations with January of the preceding year, commenting on significant changes. During February, he might present a simple month and to-date statement, together with a summary of individual products performance. For the March report, there might be a comparison of the first quarter figures to the forecast and to the same quarter for the preceeding year.

In any of these presentations, the significant variances will be discussed, and, where necessary, separate detail will be presented on them.

Since we have diverse interests represented in the meeting, we try to cover each one of them in depth throughout the year — production, laboratory, engineering, and sales. The self-interests of these separate departments help to enliven the proceedings.

Each division makes a report once a year to the corporate management committee. This is made up of the president, the vice presidents of finance, engineering, research, sales, and foreign operations, and the group vice presidents.

The divisional presentation constitutes a major review and planning effort. Each division first prepares a "book" which details operations for the current year with a comparison-to-forecast and with a new forecast for the coming year. This book usually contains a general statement by the division vice president, a financial report, a sales report, a production report, an engineering report, a report on research, and a number of individual product reports. Copies of the book are distributed to the corporate management committee two weeks before the oral presentation by the division vice president. This gives the corporate committee a chance to review the material and formulate any questions that anyone might want to raise.

At the oral presentations, each member of the division's management committee is expected to report or expand on some facet of the material contained in the written reports. This was deliberately arranged to give each person an opportunity to present a story of his operations to the overall company management. This is a means of developing our managers for higher responsibility.

Since the full presentations are contained in the books before the members of the corporate management committee, the oral presentations are confined to salient points. They depend heavily on the use of visuals displayed on an overhead proejector.

Selective Information Needs

Each level of management has its own information needs, different in detail and emphasis from level above and below it. At the top management level, data presentations must enable management to review and formulate policy and long-range plans. Top management is interested in the total earnings position of the company and the contributions of each of its divisions and product lines to the earnings position.

As the other extreme, the first-line manager is more concerned with the here and now. He must be kept informed on the specifics, on the immediate occurrences — units produced, unit costs, man-hours expended, down time, overtime, quarterly reports, etc. His most direct concern is with the operational matters on a day-to-day basis that fall within his immediate jurisdiction.

The scale of management, from top to bottom, can be a long one, so we will merely generalize in terms of a hypothetical intermediate manager. He is a man in the middle. To his superiors, he must talk in terms of dollar returns on investment and long-range plans. From his subordinates he must obtain information on the specifics of daily operation, particularly to relate individual product lines and activities to the profit picture. As a man in the middle, he must be financially "bilingual," interpreting one level to the other, both coming and going. In part, he does this through a chain of meetings linked to financial reporting.

Typically, there is no end to the amount of information you can present to management. There is, however, a limit to how much management can absorb and how many things it can act upon at any given time. Hence, reporting must be as selective in its content as possible. You can be much more inclusive in preparing the quarterly or annual book. In it, you can maintain the continuity of various time series. What you try to present in a meeting, however, is another thing. Here, you are fighting for immediate attention in competition with other information to be received in a very brief time. Either you make your point then and there or you miss it.

There are two main categories of reports. One is the performance report and the other is the information report. The performance report may also be called an "accountability report." It tells management about actual results as compared to expectations. It motivates the reporter to do the best job possible in anticipation of being held accountable.

The information report, on the other hand, should provide a basis for further planning and progress. Since there is practically no end to information, a good rule to follow is not to present anything which you cannot interpret and relate to some future policy or action potential of the company. This doesn't mean that you abandon information that you do not understand. Rather, it means that by the time you get into a meeting, you should have done the preliminary staff work that will give communicable meaning to your facts.

Of the two categories of financial report, give priority to performance or accountability information. If you have time left over, you can then move on to less imperative information.

One of the changes that has been taking place in financial reporting finds the accountant beginning to abandon — at least for his oral presentations — the big spread sheets with masses of data in which we had to search for significance. There simply is no need for this. If a man is concentrating on operating costs and has to report that everything is in line except salesmen's costs, why break out all other costs? Why not concentrate on making a quick comparison of salesmen's costs with all the others? The same holds true for other areas.

But let me, again, illustrate what I mean with the assistance of visual aids.

Suppose for a moment that you, as controller of ABC Company, must explain to management why net profit decreased during a given period despite the fact that sales were up. Using a series of simple visuals you could trace this problem to its source in a few relatively easy steps.

First, you would project a summary P and L sheet (Figure 1). Here management can readily see that the rise in sales was significantly offset by a coincident rise in manufacturing costs. Step two would be to project a visual displaying a breakdown of manufacturing costs (Figure 2), which clearly indicates that waste costs were way out of line for the period under consideration. Further analyzing the problem, you would project a waste statement (Figure 3) for the period. Immediately, you see that the waste converting operation for Product

"B" experienced a very large increase in costs. Finally, you could pinpoint the problem with a visual (Figure 4) depicting the precise area in which the trouble originated. Of course, you could go into further detail, but I believe these illustrations are sufficient to demonstrate how this technique works.

As in any situation, there are undoubtedly a host of factors in the overall P and L statement that could have engaged the attention of ABC Company's managers. However, you had a specific goal in mind — a specific message to convey — and you did not want to be sidetracked. With the use of such visual aids you, and those with whom you were communicating, could immediately begin to analyze.

So basically, you've got to start out with a simplified statement that shows the important areas in your particular business. You then can point out what areas have a problem — or appear to have a problem — and then expand it.

Maybe labor costs went up. But where did they go up? That's what the manager will want to know. Percentage figures in the various labor areas will tell you in a minute. Last time it took "X" percentage

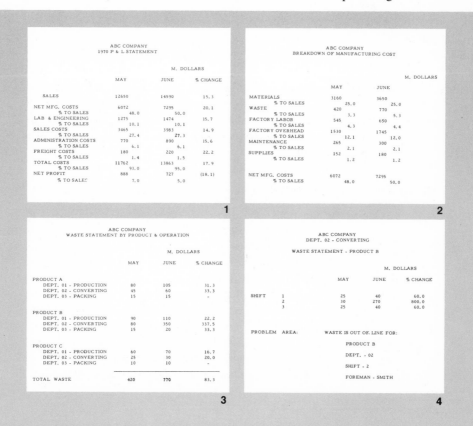

to do this; now it is taking "Y" percentage to do it. You can go through an analysis like that in a complicated situation and simplify it in a very short period to time.

Financial people preparing presentations have to remember that they want the viewer to concentrate on what is important and not waste his attention span on what is not important. Any businessman will tell you that his biggest problem is that he has too much to read, to assimilate, and too little time in which to do it. That is why it is so important for financial people to have their presentations well-planned, to the point, so that everyone will leave the meeting knowing exactly what you said.

The accountant at a management meeting must remember that he is not there to conduct an accounting course. He might amaze and delight other accountants with the niceties of fiscal details, but if he talks over the heads of management people he will have wasted time.

Financial Reporting as an Organizational Product

One of the advantages of the meeting as a tool of management is that it provides a common focus for diversity. The full potential of the financial report or presentation is not realized unless it brings operating managers and fiscal analysts into concerted effort. A few examples of this will be given here.

Teamwork in a Presentation

One of the functions of a divisional management committee is to approve price changes and to establish prices on new products. This is usually preceded by a series of meetings. The controller first calls a meeting with the laboratory to get the opinions of its personnel on the present status of the product, compared to long-range possibilities. How will any contemplated changes affect costs? A meeting with the engineering department is conducted to bring out estimates of current design and tooling costs, as well as future costs. From the meeting with production, information on the manufacturing operations is interpreted from a cost standpoint. Finally, the controller wants to know about the play of the marketplace — how pricing changes may affect estimated sales volume. For this, a meeting is held with the sales department.

The controller acts as coordinator in assembling this information and in developing its presentation to the management committee. In the actual presentation he is lead spokesman, but each member of the group is encouraged to comment on his portion of the subject and to be a party to the final decision.

Project Reporting

The project or brand management system is in widespread use. It also presents certain problems which are equally widespread. These grow out of the practice of designating one person to be in charge of an engineering development or of a new product line. As project manager, he is given total responsibility. He is expected to bring whatever resources are needed into play, even though they are not directly under his immediate responsibility. That is, he may have diversified resources directly under him, and he may also need to turn to others for support.

This system of management serves as a breeding ground for future management personnel. The project manager might be selected from any area of business — research, engineering, production, or sales.

Such a system is in operation at the 3M Company, as it is in many other organizations. The controller serves as a unifying force through his close coordination with the project manager. He serves in some respects as a balance wheel. For example, if the project manager came out of engineering, his natural tendency would be to solve all his problems through engineering. He may want engineers in the factory doing the production job, or put them in the laboratory to do research. He may even convince himself that his product is so different he must have engineers out selling it.

The controller enjoys a singularly neutral position. He doesn't manage or direct. He merely gathers the facts and interprets them. His influence on the project manager is seen in the earliest stages after the establishment of a new project activity. Very soon after his appointment, the project manager is expected to give a report on his project to the division management committee; the measure of his progress is revealed in his presentation. Long before that presentation, the controller should have been in close coordination first with the project manager, and later with his key people, in anticipation of the first and later presentations to management. At the management meeting, two reports will be made: a complete financial report by the controller and a project report by the manager in the form of an opening statement on general status and specific reports from research, engineering, production, and sales.

The Competitive Element

As a stimulus both to action and to performance analysis, the comparative report has a time-honored status. There are many variations. For example, there is the simple ranking of the profitability of product lines. Similarly, there is the ranking of individual performance by salesmen handling identical product lines. Field branches may be ranked comparatively. Performance may be compared with the same period a year ago, with the preceding period, and with forecasts or expectations. These are merely illustrative of the comparative approach.

The value of comparative reporting is in the analysis and in the action which this stimulates. In any ranking, why are the high units different than the average, what distinguishes the low units? Comparing the extremes may be fruitful, for they constitute a sharpening of differences. Such probing leads to a comparison of conditions as well as results. Sometimes you find that the poor performers may be doing exceptionally well considering the conditions under which they operate. You might also find that the top performers should be doing even better, in the light of their operating conditions.

The knowledge that relative performers will be analyzed and evaluated and that positive management action will ensue serves as a stimulus to self-improvement. On the other hand, if the reports in the big book or in the management meeting provoke no response, their stimulus value becomes largely dissipated.

Techniques of Data Presentation

The techniques with which we are here concerned are those which form the basis of oral discussion. Details can be added to the periodic reports which form the record of performance without making them voluminous. Even though they are selective, a greater degree of precision is called for, as compared to an oral presentation supported by visual aids.

Data Simplification

The suggestions that follow are intended to make financial and statistical reports a little less loaded with numbers. Of course, you must be careful not to overdo this. As you move up the line of management, you find increasing sophistication in the understanding and interpretation of numerical symbols. Consider the following, when appropriate:

1. Round out figures to the nearest hundreds, thousands, millions, or billions. Long complicated numbers are not readily grasped. You can appropriately express $3,507,314.72 as $3,500,000.

2. Drop final digits in favor of words. The preceding number might also be expressed as "3-1/2" or "3.5 million dollars." In a tabular presentation, you can save numbers by stating at the head of a column: "To nearest hundreds, thousands, or millions." Figures should be grouped for ready comparison in tabular form. If they are spread through a paragraph, they are difficult to follow.

Data Charting

There is a distinct trend away from the elaborate chart that looks as if it had been made up by a professional artist. There is a definite place for these, as in annual reports and other public documents, but for internal use, a "quickie" visual has certain advantages over a finished chart. The "quickie" has a freehand appearance. It is not sloppy. Rather, it approaches what is called an "artist's rough," a sketch which an artist would make before he prepares a finished chart.

Actually, the freehand appearance conveys more of a sense of timeliness. It does so quite literally, for such a visual can be more up to the moment that one that has had to compete its way through the art shop. If you are reporting to management on the cost of the latest run or if you are presenting an estimate of the month's operations before the final figures are in, the quickie will actually seem more to the moment.

Aim to bring out key relationships. Often, these can be expressed in very simple terms. Numbers in themselves are not significant. Rather, it is the relationship of one number from one source to another number from a different source that matters. Of course, this assumes that there is an inherent relationship to begin with. The situation may seem to be quite complex, yet the challenge in designing a presentation is to identify the essentials in a situation and to reduce them to simple terms.

A visual aid should stand on its own. That is, while it may be elaborated upon in discussions as well as in supporting documents, it should largely be self-explanatory. A good visual aid embodies the following three elements:

1. A simple caption or sentence that states the informational goal of the chart — what it shows;

2. A simple graphic visualization of the relationships to be brought out in the chart;

3. Subsidiary identifications or "pointers" that emphasize key points, trends, relationships, levels, etc.

Studies of responses to different types of graphic presentations have brought out a few simple rules of effective communication of data. In essence, the easiest charts to follow are bar charts and pie charts. In contrast, line graphs and surface charts are much more difficult to follow, in that order. These observations were brought out as a result of studies conducted by faculty members of the University of Wisconsin. The relevant techniques and explanations of them are shown in the illustrations and captions that follow this chapter.

In the physical preparation of the material, remember to conform to the proportions of the projection medium — overhead projector or slide projector — if either is used; 35mm slides are in the proportions of 2" × 3" (conforming to the slide format of 24 × 36mm). Transparencies prepared in an office copying machine use 8-1/2 × 11-inch film and original materials are made up in that size.

The overhead projector has a glass stage or "table top" on which the transparency is placed. The speaker can see his chart, well-illuminated as it lies on the glass stage. A pencil, or any other pointer touched to the transparency will be projected as a pointer on the screen. This introduces an element of motion to guide the viewer.

Certain charts can be set up at the beginning of the year with grid lines, headings, and legends inked in. Actual performance or trend lines can be added each month with tape, or overlays can be used to show succeeding results or to compare past and present performance.

For variety, use some "negative" visuals occasionally. Here, the illustrations show up in reverse as white lines and figures on a black background instead of the customary black-on-white. Negatives stand out conspicuously and dramatically. Since they may be a little hard on the eyes if you show too many, the technique should be used sparingly.

Mr. Andrew G. Beck, Assistant Vice President, The Central Trust Company of Cincinnati, Ohio, is a confirmed user of visual aids, who also has a preference for the overhead projector. He has built financial presentations around the ease with which projection transparencies can be made.

He uses the revelation technique to prevent the audience from running ahead of his presentation. A sheet of paper is placed over the transparency to cover everything except that which he wants the audience to see at that moment. As the discussion moves along, he lowers the sheet of paper on the transparency to permit more information to be projected.

This point-by-point disclosure prevents his audience from jumping to erroneous conclusions. The last line should be read last, not first.

As a variation of this, Mr. Beck starts with a base transparency, and adds overlays, each of which contains additional information. Mr. Beck used overlays, for example, to show a 10-year picture of growth at his bank. His base transparency is in the form of a blank graph, with only the dates on the bottom and the figures on the side. He then adds to this chart another transparency which shows the level of undivided profits for each year. The bars of this chart are made of transparent yellow tape. Then he adds another transparency on which bars of blue tape show capital growth. Surplus is shown with red bars in the same way, and finally, another transparency is added to show capital accounts with strips of transparent green tape to make the bars.

When he wants to make line graphs, he uses special pencils, felt pens, and other accessories. Over the years, he has used this technique before hundreds of audiences in and out of the bank.

I

**Use Labels on Elements
Instead of a Key:**
Graphs are clearer when each bar
is identified by a label right
on the bar.

II

**Place Figures on Elements
Instead of Using a Grid:**
Graphs are clearer when quantitative
differences are shown as numerals
on the bars themselves.

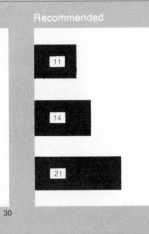

III

**Use Segmented Bars
Rather Than Surface Charts:**
The surface chart at the left is easy
to draw, but of all graphs it is hardest
for readers in estimating or comparing
quantities. Unless the full details of
the trend are required, comparisons
expressed in separate bars
are better.

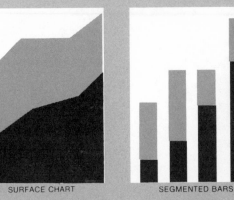

SURFACE CHART   SEGMENTED BARS

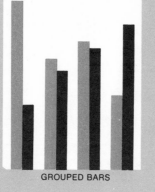

LINE GRAPHS

GROUPED BARS

Use Grouped Bars IV
Rather Than Line Graphs:
For estimating or comparing quantities,
the grouped bar chart (right)
is preferable.

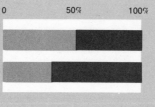

0   50%   100%

Pie Charts Are Just as Good V
as Percentage Bar Graphs:
Pie charts and percentage bar
charts are about equally functional
for portraying divisions of 100 percent. The bar chart is generally the
easier to design.

Vertical Bars Are Just as Good VI
as Horizontal Bars:
Bars can be placed either vertically
or horizontally on a chart with little
significant difference in reader compre-
hension. However, a horizontal bar
chart has the advantage of allowing
more room for labeling each bar
with names and figures.

Notes

Chapter X

Staff Meetings: Boon or Bore?

It's pleasure to attend a good staff meeting. You leave with a feeling that you have observed teamwork in action.

If your pleasure may be likened to the relief or sudden surcease from pain or discomfort, it is because most staff meetings are a bore. This is unfortunate, for with just a little effort they can become a boon to all concerned.

From an organizational standpoint, the staff meeting brings the fragmented group together to have its unity recharged. The staff meeting provides an opportunity to accomplish five aspects of the well-rounded communication program. These five points have been identified by Lawrence Appley, former president of the American Management Association, as follows:

1. transmitting ideas or decisions;
2. clarifying an idea or problem;
3. getting participation in developing a solution to the problem;
4. motivating others to take action agreed upon;
5. measuring the effectiveness of communication.

Why do staff meetings often fall flat? What is wrong with them? In any single case, the reasons may vary, but they are likely to be found among the following:

Staff meetings may be conducted routinely even when there is nothing of real interest on the agenda;

Staff meetings are conducted without being linked to an action system which includes preparation as well as followup;

Staff meetings are conducted by supervisory personnel who have not been uniformly trained in effective conduct of meetings;

Staff meetings are conducted too frequently;

Staff meetings sometimes last too long.

Formula for Effective Staff Meetings

The successful staff meeting must be a way of life; it needs to be part of an outgoing system. This can be expressed as a set of rules:

1. Hold staff meetings regularly, but not more often than necessary for worthwhile communication.

2. Balance the agenda of the staff meeting with both performance reporting and information reporting.

3. Make the staff meeting a vital link in an action system.

Of course, there are other important ingredients which influence success or failure, not the least of which is the manner in which the meeting is conducted.

Frequency of Staff Meetings

Some administrators are staunch advocates of the staff meeting. They hold regular weekly meetings with each of their division heads. They meet separately with division heads and the staff of the latter. They believe this brings them in close relationship with as many of the staff as possible.

The division head becomes overburdened with meetings. He participates with other division heads in the regular weekly meeting of the administrator, as already noted. He holds his own staff meeting, which is attended by the administrator, also as noted above. Then, because he and his staff cannot talk as freely as they would like when the administrator is present, he holds an additional staff meeting without the administrator!

That's a lot of meetings in any man's week. Besides, there are quite a few more at subordinate levels we haven't covered. You can imagine the aggregate cost of all this communication. If the meetings accomplished something really worthwhile, they would be a good investment. But the value of their return is questionable. Before each meeting, a secretary calls around to ask what items there are for the meeting agenda. Then, there is a feverish preparation and assembly of reports to be made at the meeting. It gets held, business goes on as usual — and the same old problems that have been plaguing management continue to exist.

There are several things wrong with this situation; one of them is that there are too many meetings held too frequently. On this matter of frequency, we can break out some subsidiary rules:

a. The more routine the business, the less frequent the need for regular meetings.

b. The more dynamic the business — the more sensitive to conditions and environment — the more frequent must be the meetings.

Remember too, that it is this sensitivity which so necessitates meetings which effectively communicate. As we noted before there is a definite relationship to the successful, growing concerns and those who have discovered the meeting as a vital management tool for effective communication.

c. As a rule of thumb, regular meetings should be held about once a month — more frequently, if conditions warrant.

When the meeting is held too frequently, it tends to lose its significance. It ceases to be an event to look forward to; it becomes an occasion for reciting what has transpired, rather than an occasion for good analytical thinking. It is pretty hard to prepare analytical reports on a once-a-week basis. The meeting held too frequently tends to degenerate into an inventory of trivia. It becomes a bore.

Now there are many situations in which the once a month rule wouldn't really make enough time available for all the important subjects. If this is found regularly to be true, the meetings might have to be held more frequently, but it might be much better to hold special meetings — and to call them "special." Then, if any of the meetings is to lose its mystique, let it be the special one. One should try to retain a certain quality for the regular meeting; it should be regarded as an event for which participants carefully prepare — out of which comes the stimulus for further action of a noticeable character.

A Mixture of Action and Information

The balanced agenda should include both performance reporting and information reporting to and from the meeting leader.

From an action standpoint, the regular meeting is used as an occasion for reviewing the status of projects. This review should be preceded by thorough staff work on the part of each reporting individual. This preparation might entail subsidiary meetings between him and his supervisor and colleagues. In this way, it serves as a spur to developmental thinking in anticipation of the day when the assembled group acts as a court of review, analysis, and judgment.

The informational content should be heavily loaded with "state of the union" information from each of his staff members to help the supervisor know what is going on, and to be able to anticipate problems in the making. The staff members want information that will give them a clue as to where they are going. They want to know how their activities fit into the larger scope of the supervisor's plans and actions. They want to know, also, how particular policies and actions of the company will affect their personal status and emoluments.

Meetings Within the Framework of Action

An administrator is committing a costly error when he gets too close to his second level of subordinates. He blocks their freedom of discussion. There are always things that a supervisor and his staff like to discuss among themselves without feeling that they are under the immediate surveillance of a higher level of management. It is almost like having a hidden microphone and TV camera in the conference room.

What the administrator must try to accomplish is the establishment of a vertical chain of communication in which one staff meeting is linked to another above it and to yet another below it. This way the supervisor who conducts a staff meeting is also a participant in the meeting called by his superior. To his own subordinates, the supervisor brings back what he learned in that meeting; he brings to the meeting conducted by his superior what he learned from his subordinates. In this manner, vertical linkage is provided for communication from top to bottom of the organization. (There is also some degree of horizontal communication, but it becomes more effective toward the top of the organizational pyramid.)

What is called for is a system of goal formulating and performance accounting that links each level to the next higher one. In performance reporting, you need predetermined goals or targets established in a framework of fulfillment, with each level participating in the formulation of these goals and targets.

Subsequently, those with responsibility for execution must report (upward) both their accomplishments and the problems they have that need resolving. In a well-managed system, provision is made for this to be done on an "exception basis." Here's what this means. Routine progress is taken care of through routine reporting. Exceptional accomplishment is given special attention, particularly in staff meetings, in the form of open recognition for those who have earned it. Significant variances from target are discussed openly too, especially when they involve group judgments that have worked out badly. Getting back on the track may call for a revision of goals; sometimes, a revision of methods used to achieve goals.

If the staff meeting is tied into a total system of company-wide management accountability in this way, the staff meeting becomes a powerful management tool.

Aspects of Intimacy

The regular staff meeting brings together people who may see each other rather frequently through the days and weeks between meetings. The regular staff meeting tends to enter into the consciousness of the participants as part of the web of office behavior and politics. What one says and might say in a staff meeting may have political significance.

In this situation, the supervisor is the key figure. He sets the tone of conduct and participation.

The General Climate

Communication in the staff meeting itself can be congenial, expressive, and constructive if these attributes characterize everyday relationships and communication. The supervisor who nourishes good communication outside the meeting will have little difficulty in stimulating it when his staff is assembled. Conversely, if he stifles communication within his group or between it and himself, he cannot hope to have a spontaneous outpouring in the meeting of anything — but evidences of low morale. The most he can expect is a cautious response to mandated inquiries or requests for performance.

The day-to-day environment for fostering good communication must be characteristic of the company as a whole. This is one of the best safeguards against the ineffective supervisor; since he himself performs in this climate, he cannot help but be influenced by it.

If communication, as it is said, is a two-way street, management is often guilty of far more telling, informing, and commanding than listening, asking and interpreting. This has been brought out by numerous surveys. Management must take particular pains to listen. Not listening is tantamount to admitting it doesn't really care to learn what is on the minds of its employees. Management must listen and then it must feed back information that can be interpreted as response to what has been communicated upward.

The Supervisor As Chairman

The typical staff meeting operates at two levels of discourse. First, there is the obvious level of the official agenda, people addressing themselves to the accepted order of things. They are presumably talking in terms of the formal structure of goals and relationships. Underlying this level, however, is the inevitable vying for position that goes on constantly between the supervisor and each of his employees. Overlying everything, additionally, is the web of relationships that makes up the total pattern of good behavior. The supervisor must be particularly aware of all this as he conducts the discussion. He must know where sensitivies lie so that he can both stimulate participation and avoid tension or needless embarrassment.

Effective staff meetings call for good preparation, good chairmanship, good participation, attention to the techniques for problem solving, and visual aids.

Summary

Staff meetings need not be boring. Here are some guidelines to make them successful.

1. Frequency of meetings should follow the dictates of necessity. Routine businesses require fewer meetings. Dynamic, growing companies will be sensitive to ever-changing business conditions and will meet more regularly.

2. Agenda should include both performance reports to evaluate staff activity and informational reports to guide staff in their duties.

3. Meetings should be held on separate, chains-of-command levels

— then linked together on supervisory levels to achieve company-wide management accountability.

4. Meetings should be a two-way street with both staff and management giving and receiving information.

5. Thorough preparation and use of visual aids will shorten meeting time and result in better communication.

Notes

Chapter XI

Committee Meetings

Of all meeting groups, the committee seems most in disrepute. It is criticized as being a burial place for management problems. It is accused of diffusing and confusing executive responsibility. It is indicted for being slow and indecisive.

The committee has many legitimate roles to fulfill, nevertheless. Some companies are organized around what is called the committee system, and many make effective use of committees. There are two sides to the coin.

The probability is that when committees are not used effectively it is because they have been set up without regard to reasoned criteria that govern effective use of committees in general. The success of an individual committee depends upon good committee management practices. Building upon this base, successful performance calls for use of the general techniques that go into the conduct of an excellent meeting. In this chapter, accordingly, we will review briefly some aspects of committee organization and management.

Committee Organization

The committee is a form of activity organization which cuts across normal lines of command. It is given semi-permanent or continuing responsibility for the accomplishment of an assigned mission, just as is done with any unit of organization. Yet, it is also different in that it normally does not have a specific operating function pertaining to the production or selling of goods and services. The structure elements of a committee which we will discuss here include its general definition, its charter, its chairman, its membership, and its mechanism for secretariat service.

Definition of the Committee

The committee is a body of people who meet together on a continuing basis to accomplish an assigned mission. The committee may have a specific task to investigate and report on. Thereupon, it might be disbanded, or it might be given further tasks to execute. There are other committees which have recurrent matters brought before them, such as committees of award, committees of property survey, budget committees, retirement committees, etc.

The committee is usually set up to accomplish something that cannot be done through the existing organization. Logically, there may be no single place in which to assign that function, or the committee may afford a means of bypassing ordinary channels when these are not likely to be productive. Some will say that this violates the purity of organization. They may be correct, yet there are many situations in all enterprises in which one may be quite satisfied with the existing order while welcoming an extra means, like a committee, for the exceptional occasion when ordinary arrangements would prove unsatisfactory.

The Committee Charter

The terms of reference of a committee should be defined just as clearly as those of any other unit of organization. If it has a specific, one-time mission, that should be stated. The discharge of the committee from further responsibility should also be provided for in the original charter.

Certain committees have continuing tenure, just as do regular units of organization. The corporate management committee, for example, may be a permanent entity, varying only with changes in membership.

There may also be special budget committees, planning committees, etc. Any of these continuing committees should have their terms of reference carefully drawn so that they supplement, rather than duplicate or usurp, the continuing responsibilities of company executives.

The relationships of committees to staff and line offices should be carefully worked out and described in the original charter, as well as in supplementary documents. If this is not done, there is apt to be a fair amount of indecision and inaction due to a desire to avoid conflict. It is a good idea, before the charter document is finalized, to solicit the comments of people in the organization who are likely to be affected. Thus management can at least identify sensitivity points. These will help to sharpen the definitions of committee responsibilities, including whether it is to recommend, to decide, to take action, or merely to serve as a sounding board.

The Chairman

The single most important ingredient of committee success is its chairman. He is the man who carries the committee responsibility on a continuing basis. While he may use an executive secretary to assist him, he is the one who oversees the preparation of the agenda. He is also responsible for the discussion management of each item on the agenda. He must have attributes of a self-starter. He must have demonstrated an ability to get things done through people, particularly since committee members often need to be prodded to fulfill their contributing responsibilities.

The chairman quite often has no direct responsibility over the members of his committee. While they are expected to respond to his leadership as a matter of course, his greatest effectiveness lies in being able to command the respect of the committee membership. He must also be someone in whose judgment management will have confidence. Of course, it should go without saying that he should be someone who has demonstrated an ability to conduct a good meeting.

Committee Membership

As a general rule, the membership of a committee should be broadly inclusive of all interests which it is supposed to represent; neither functional interest nor point-of-view interests should be omitted from representation. This does not mean that you overload the boat. It puts a greater emphasis on committee selection to make sure that it is adequate in its coverage. If the committee is to make decisions by which others in the organization must abide, committee membership is regarded by them as evidence of fair judgment.

The size of the committee will vary. Any tendency to represent all interests will push the committee membership higher than functional discussion should permit. Accordingly, a conscious counter-effort should be undertaken to limit committee size. For this, one can't really use a rule of thumb, because the functions, problem characteristics, and organizational characteristics will have a lot to do with membership.

Since the committee will operate on a continuing basis, the members should be selected with regard to their mutual compatibility. On the other hand, if they get along too well, or if they tend to think alike too much, they might not have enough of the constructive conflict that leads to good analysis, problem solving, and decision. Therefore, it might be deliberately determined in some cases to include some abrasive elements in a committee's membership. As a general rule, committee members should be of approximately equal status. This will minimize the risk of members being inhibited by the superior status of others or, in reverse, of individual members taking advantage of their senior roles.

Individual dependability is another important element in selection. In the ordinary situation in which a supervisor is in charge of a meeting, the conventional means of disciplining performance are available. In a committee, the chairman might have to spend entirely too much of his time getting people to be prepared and to come to meetings promptly without having direct disciplinary authority to accomplish this. In order to conserve his time and to avoid embarrassment, people who are known not to be dependable for service on a committee should be avoided. Of course, sometimes you can't tell until you have tried a man.

The Committee Secretary

Although one normally starts with the selection of a committee chairman, it is sometimes a good idea to have in mind at the same time the committee member who acts as secretary. The two must form a good working team. You can sometimes sacrifice some qualities in a chairman, for example, if you know that you have just the right kind of dynamic secretary who will attend to an agenda and otherwise make sure that the business of the committee moves along. It could very well be that you want as chairman a man who has an exceptional status in the organization who can also run a good meeting. It can be tacitly understood that the other burdens of committee work will fall on the secretary. When this is the case, however, the secretary should realize that he must protect the operating "front" of his chairman. He must not give a public or conspicuous impression that he is the one who is running the committee. In fact, he is not, for he is obliged to seek the guidance and review of his chairman, and to operate accordingly.

The committee secretary should be one who has a demonstrated ability to organize a project, to work on the development of agenda topics, to express himself effectively on paper, to produce the paperwork and reports of the committee, and to maintain good contact with the members of the committee as well as with those who have business before it. He must, in short, be the one who helps assure that the committee business gets done. Often, he is the continuing spirit of the committee if it should change its chairman over a period of time.

Dynamic Maintenance of the Committee

Over a period of time committees tend to perpetulate themselves. Most committees should have specific assignments, after which they should go out of business. But committees tend to find reasons to continue. Hence it is well to provide in the original charter for the automatic demise of committees which should be assigned definite life spans. One way of doing this is to provide that unless the committee's life is extended through positive action, it will automatically go out of business.

It is sometimes a good idea to provide generally for review of committee purpose and membership at stated intervals. This tends to keep the committee alert to its own internal dynamics. It helps assure that committees are pursuing worthwhile objectives. Just as original purposes of regular organizational units may no longer be viable, so may there need to be a restructuring of committee arrangements.

Rotation of committee membership serves a triple purpose: providing management with fresh viewpoints; energizing the committee by disturbing complacencies of thinking; and giving more people an opportunity for management development through participation in committee activities.

Additional mileage in the form of organizational communication may sometimes be derived from committee work. Let's suppose an important technical or organizational paper is prepared for a committee and the thinking contained in that paper is of broad value to the company. The secretary should be charged with distributing such a document on a need-to-know basis. The same pertains to committee reports. On the other hand, these should not be so freely distributed as to give no distinction to them. The rule to be maintained is *"need to know."*

Summary

The success of an individual committee will depend upon good management practices. Here are some guidelines to follow:

1. The role and responsibility of a committee should be clearly defined. It should not usurp responsibilities of company executives. The relationship between committee and staff should be clear. Sensitivity points in this area should be examined.

2. The committee's length of tenure should be specifically stated.

3. The committee should understand what action it is expected to take.

4. Committee chairman must be a self-starter who can get things done and command respect.

5. Committee should be representative of all points of interest. However, size should be kept in bounds.

6. Members should be of approximately equal status.

7. Committee secretary should have ability as project organizer.

8. Rotation of committee members desirable for fresh viewpoints in standing committees.

9. Committee should be disbanded after it has served its purpose.

Notes

Notes

The Sales Spectacular

"The lonelist job in the business world." That's how a seasoned and sympathetic sales manager recently described the life of a salesman in the field.

The beginning paragraphs of an article in a midwestern newspaper set a similar tone:

"No. No. No. No. No. No. No. No. No. No.

"If you've heard that unpleasant word addressed to you ten or more times a day, know what it's like to drive your car around the block three or four times before you muster up the courage to make that call, if your wife doesn't always understand why you may have to work at night, if your boss, 100 or 1,000 miles away, doesn't understand your problems, if your mind is cluttered up with bills, costs, quotas, promotions, closings and the competition — and you have nobody to commiserate with — then you very well might be one of the thousands of on-the-street salesmen who live in this area.

"And if that isn't a dismal enough daily routine to look forward to, you also have to put up with the all too prevalent salesman's image; the fast-talking, fast-buck nightrider out to skin one and all. The image, for the most part, is about as outdated as Grandma's bloomers but like old wives' tales, it dies reluctantly."

Salesmen are the lifeblood of every business organization. But those in the field, away from their home offices, do lead lonely existences. They lack the comradery, the companionship that others centrally located in business can count on to lead them through difficult or annoying daily situations. Company communications, though often, are usually impersonal letters, sales directives, memos. Cold communication.

They for the most part are all alone and on their own. They must exert a self-discipline that others do not. It is their own self-discipline that gets them up in the morning, without supervision, and out on the road. They must have thick skins and great amounts of perseverance to rebuff the ten or more "no's" they may meet with each day.

A sales management specialist put it this way: "One of the basic problems in the trade is what we call no-itus. They've heard that word, NO, so much they get hypnotized by it and come to expect it. So you see that one of the biggest problems in sales is maintaining a positive attitude. In fact, the first rule is to believe unto yourself. But this belief is a wandering thing. Some months it's there and other months it's not there at all."

The sales expert continued, "Frankly 50 per cent of our efforts is to get their attitude right, then you teach them the skills. We tell them that 80 per cent of success lies in their attitude toward themselves, their customers and their product and only 20 per cent in product knowledge. A guy can have fantastic product knowledge, but if he never leaves the house what good is it?"

Even to the most thick-skinned the effects of being told "No" repeatedly can be psychologically devastating.

Attitude. Motivation. Comradery. These are probably the chief rationale factors behind the decision to hold a sales spectacular. It is an attempt to combine business with pleasure. To let the salesmen in the field know their company is concerned with them and their problems, give them a chance to meet their compatriots in other parts of the country and exchange problems and solutions, let them blow off a little stream, have some fun, and at the same time introduce them to new products or company moves and examine how they react to it all. In essence, let them know that they are not really all alone. As the lyrics to a popular tune puts it, "We're all playing in the same band. . ."

The rise-and-shine or hoot-and-holler sales meeting is in a class by itself. It is the nearest thing in business to a showman's extravaganza and sometimes it compares with the best from the fantasy world of the impresario.

Underneath the veneer of gags, humor, carnival costumes, and even imported entertainers, an underlying note of seriousness must pervade and prevail. There is no mistaking that those present are there because the survival of the business depends on the making of sales. One sales executive calls this type a "carrot-and-stick" meeting.

What's different about the sales meeting extravaganza?

1. It is heavy on showmanship, partly to build up a sense of anticipation before the meeting and partly to maintain interest and provide light relief for a meeting that lasts one or more full days.

2. It calls for a heavy investment of money and time. It costs a great deal to put on a big sales meeting. No small part of this is the cost of taking men away from their selling activities — time which they must make up after the sales meeting.

3. It involves a tremendous amount of planning for program, preparation of speakers, preparation of exhibits, travel arrangements, entertainment when used, meeting room arrangements, etc.

The formula for a successful sales meeting is advance planning coupled with meticulous follow-through that continues until the very last minute of the last item on the agenda.

Multi-Media

One of the more popular formats for the sales spectacular today goes by the various names of Mixed-Media, Multi-Media, Total Theater, etc. Whatever the name, the technique is designed to combine or commingle the various instruments of audio-visual, live presentation, room design and props to achieve the greatest impact to the senses of SIGHT, SOUND and TOUCH. The Multi-Media technique usually employs the story writing technique of theme which hopefully leads to a dramatic, mind-changing, conclusion.

In a special edition, *Sales Meetings Magazine* described how some of the various audio-visual media can be used for multi-media effect:

35mm Slide Projector: Can be used to project with other projectors simultaneous images, or as a flashing light source that can be focused. Using a zoom lens, projected image can be varied before, during and after images are projected.

To add zest, you can set up a fourth projector with a tray of kinetic slides and project the images on the audience. Kinetic slides contain geometric designs.

Slide Projector Accessories: Kodak's polarizing unit can be attached to the front of a slide projector. Unit contains a screen wheel which rotates in front of the projector lens. Slides contain a special polarized film created by Technamations, Inc. Combination creates both a stationary projected image and parts which simulate movement.

Other accessory devices include those which permit you to vary the rate of speed at which slides are shown, or electro-mechanical devices to control two or more projectors and tape recorders simultaneously from one pre-programmed control center. Many of these systems also include fade and dissolve mechanisms which eliminate the 1/5th second of blank screen while slides are being changed.

Motion Picture Projectors: Aside from the obvious use of projecting a moving image on one of your screens, you can mix projection dramatically for your multi-media scheme. For instance, try projecting a loop film continuously on the ceiling. Loop is a short piece of film that travels continuously through the projector.

Overhead Projectors: These are used to create liquid light. By placing vegetable dyes into vegetable oils in a glass pie pan, constant moving and changing color forms are projected. There are innumerable combinations of images that can be simply produced by adding revolving discs of moire patterns, color wheels and diffraction discs over the lens.

Light Machines: Besides using the projector as a light machine, there are also regular light machines available which are designed specifically to set a tone and atmosphere in an environment. These units are similar to those used in a theater.

Stroboscopic Light Units: A strobe is a high intensity flashing light that can create dream-like images. Or, they can be used to create disorientation. Strobes are essentially attention-getting devices that must be used carefully in order not to turn the audience off.

Color Sound Boxes: Electronic unit couples colored lamps with music. Rhythm and loudness of music controls various colored lamps.

Ultra Violet Light: This is also called black light and is available in both fluorescent and incandescent fixtures.

Dichromatic Spotlights: These commercially available spotlights have two colors in each bulb. When used with a blinker attachment, they create pulsating color shadows.

Spotlights: These theatrical spotlights are easily available. When used unconventionally, spots are effective in expanding the environment and involving the audience. Color wheel and silhouette shapes can be attached.

Projection Surfaces: While portable beaded screens are considered standard projection surfaces, multi-media expands to include every surface in the meeting room: walls, floor ceiling and people.*

Sales Meetings also described how one firm used what is called the Total Theater approach to lessen the tedium of hearing an extensive series of speeches. The presentation was broken up with skits, jingles, songs and dances which were interjected between the speeches at desired moments. In this case both live and recorded music were used. The speakers appeared at one podium and the cast at the other. Spotlights were used to highlight the speakers or the cast according to whom was performing at the time. Slides were shown from three high-powered Carousel projectors.

The company sales manager commented at the conclusion: "We thought the program was excellent. However, the Total Theater concept could be disastrous unless it is used judiciously. Whether you use skits, songs or jingles depends on what you are trying to achieve or say. We didn't try to overdo it. Rather than bombard the audience, we entertainingly informed them."

Multi-media should indeed be used judiciously. Stanford Sobel, writing in *Business Screen* magazine compared Multi-Media with public reaction to the first motion pictures. "It was sheer magic — but the novelty wore off. The same applies to Multi-Media. A lot may look on Multi-Media as magic — pure magic — but others, and their number is increasing geometrically — are becoming annoyed by the monotony — pure monotony — of the Multi-Media presentations they see.

"In Montreal (the Exposition) the public learned that there is no reason for Multi-Media to depend solely upon the magic of moving images. They also can have content and that content can be exciting as format.

"It certainly is an unqualified fact that the closer the form represents the inner content of the material the more successful the Multi-Media presentation will communicate."

Sobel concluded, "It now is an accepted fact that the outer expression (the hardware) should be a true projection of the inner feeling tone(the subject matter). Magic alone is no longer enough."

Mr. Sobel's views strongly parallel my own in this regard. Audio-Visuals can distract as well as emphasize. They should not become of such prime importance that content is subordinated, that the sales executive who needs the meeting loses control of it. Even the best multi-media show in the world will fail if it doesn't say something.

It is my observation in this respect that in many cases, the more

*Reprinted with permission from SALES MEETINGS magazine

money a manager or a division or a region spends on a meeting, and the more gaudy it is, the more fuzzy is its purpose. The manager who is calling the meeting is not sure how to get his message across so he resorts to the philosophy which says, "If you have nothing to say, snow them with noise and sophistication."

One should always keep in mind the costs of such spectaculars. When a salesman is attending a meeting he is not out selling. One rule of thumb states that if a company is operating at a 10 per cent profit margin and conducts a sales meeting which costs $100,000, sales will have to increase $1,000,000 to cover that cost.

Planning for a Sales Meeting

From planning through final execution, there is an endless stream of detail to be managed. Any single small detail can make the difference between success and frustration. Hence, you do not rush into a sales meeting. You allow yourself time to plan, to develop, to check on yourself, and then to check some more.

There are a few key decisions which will govern the overall character and conduct of your sales meeting. We'll go into these here. For case studies of the experiences of others and for checklists governing every aspect of meeting preparation, there are supplementary sources which the reader might care to consult. One, to which I have already referred, is *Sales Meetings Magazine*. Two books on the subject are Joseph D. Cooper's *Handbook for Sales Meetings, Conventions and Conferences and How to Make Them Work* (The National Sales Development Institute, Division of Prentice-Hall, Inc., Waterford, Connecticut) and Bill N. Newman's *Handbook of Successful Sales Meetings* (Prentice-Hall, Inc., Englewood Cliffs, New Jersey).

The Purpose of the Meeting

Before you can decide anything else, you must be clear as to the *specific* goal of your meeting. Now you begin shaping up a tentative program, from which you can determine whether you want a single national sales meeting or a series of regional sales meetings, depending perhaps on a single controlling factor, such as the difficulty of shipping a large quantity of delicate equipment around the country from one location to another within a short span of time. Once you make this decision, you can then concentrate on other aspects of meeting planning.

Looking at your generalized goals — do you want mainly to inspire and stimulate the sales organization? If so, you might best conduct a single national meeting at which you would have exhibits, demonstrations, speakers, and a fast pace of whoop-de-doo! While you want feedback from the attendees at a sales meeting, this becomes a secondary goal, to be achieved through a series of subsidiary meetings, perhaps, in which the participants are broken up into smaller groups for discussion purposes.

On the other hand, if your aim is to promote a great deal of discussion, if you want to be able to identify intimately with as many members of the field sales organization as possible, you might consider having a series of regional meetings. These provide better opportunities to develop personal working relationships and to have members of your staff set up the informal ties that later will pay off in innumerable ways.

More on Regional vs. National Meetings

The most expensive part of a sales meeting is the time that the participants take away from actual selling. They've got to make up for that lost time and then some.

You are much more likely to get good attendance at non-compulsory meetings such as dealer meetings when they are conducted as close as possible to the home bases of the participants. You cut down on their travel time as well as on their expenses. For you, however, the expenses go up tremendously. The 3M Company has found out that it spends three times as much to conduct seven regional sales meetings as it does to conduct one national meeting at a central place. What the regional sales groups and dealers save in time, we lose several times over. We take a big cut of our national staff's work time. You might feel that this is to be expected of sales management personnel, but we also bring in people for the meeting, from engineering and from other departments, who normally have very little to do with selling but who do leave other work to attend.

Nevertheless, we tend toward the decentralized meeting. We have a rule of thumb never to have more than fifty people in a room. This makes for a more intimate relationship, and it permits us to have more of a crossfire of discussion. We are also better able to make use of a working type of visual presentation medium, such as the overhead projector.

Detail Planning

Once you have determined the theme and general outline of the meeting format, you must begin to work up more detailed plans which leave nothing to chance. Each of the key functionaries at headquarters should be solicited for program suggestions. So should the regional sales managers and participants in the meetings. Long before this type of planning gets under way, however, you need to have an idea of budget. This is conditioned in the first instance by what you feel is the general outline of the sales meeting. Nevertheless, there are budgetary limits which may oblige you to fashion the meeting to come within your means. The budget must be subdivided and then communicated to all those who are required to live within it. The budget, incidentally, also serves as one of your tools of planning. While it might start out as an overall estimate, it is gradually solidified by translating each element of the projected meeting into an estimated cost.

Execution of the Meeting

There are two major categories into which you can group all of the meeting details. One is everything pertaining to program development and execution. The other is everything pertaining to physical arrangements. This suggests a possible subdivision for purposes of delegation. You can, of course, subdivide even further, in order to have more people working on the plan. This will depend upon how elaborate your meeting is and how many people are available to assist. Remember, though, that the execution of a meeting is not something you can leave to a clerk. The logistics must be exceptionally precise. While you can learn a great deal from the experiences of others communicated to you directly or through books and articles, in the final analysis, in order to acquire that sixth sense that tells you what booby traps to avoid, you must personally have lived through the alarms, pitfalls, and frustrations of actual sales meetings.

Program Content

The secret of success in program development is the detailed plan — a blueprint that leaves nothing to the imagination. It is explicit as to goals and sub-goals. It identifies the speakers and what each is supposed to accomplish within an allotted time. It lists the props each will need and identifies those who are to prepare them in accordance with scheduled deadlines.

The massed outline serves as a flexible tool of planning. It guides rehearsals and, from experiences at these, it undergoes change. Last-minute details are plugged into the outline also, so that at any time there will be one central source of information on every aspect of the sales meeting.

Rehearsals are vital. They should be monitored by at least some people who do not feel it necessary to be agreeable. It must be remembered that a sales meeting is a presentation and that a sales meeting is for selling something. You must not be carried away by the showmanship. You might think that you have a great meeting merely because you have spectacular entertainment. Sometimes, you might be disappointed to learn that you might just as well have sent everyone to the movies at much less expense.

Writing in *Sales Management*, Mr. Charles H. Brennan of N. W. Ayer & Son, Inc., of Philadelphia, commented on some of the pitfalls in three types of sales spectaculars.

The first is comedy. Played before a captive audience, the risk of comedy is that it may lose the audience before the main business is put across. "Humor," says Brennan, "is a delicate thing at best. One man's laugh is another man's wince. If you must be funny, know your group intimately."

The humorous presentation is tough to organize or pace properly. Too many digressions.

"If the presentation is really humorous, the audience tends to remember the laughs and forget the message.

"Excessive informality and familarity can be very annoying, if not downright distasteful."

The sermon is the opposite pole of presentation mood. After being down the paths of righteousness and salvation for an hour or so, the typical listener is more apt to be concerned with escape than with wondering what the constructive guidance is likely to be, especially if the logic of the presentation is utterly unrelated to the sales appeals for which the listeners are hopefully waiting.

The Broadway musical-type extravaganza has so much invested in it that its producers live in mortal fear of a dismal flop. The great danger is that the basic theme and the specific messages of sales technique may get lost in the shuffle when the meeting tends toward show biz rather than sales biz.

Here are some of the ingredients of success:

1. *Simplification.* Each nut or bolt you can take out is that much less to go wrong.

2. *Rehearsal.* Check on everything. Keep on doing so up until the very last minute.

3. *Timing.* Don't make estimates for other people based on your own experiences. Grand rehearsals should bring all elements of timing together. When you use outside speakers, you must be sure they know all about your timing requirements.

4. *Varied pace.* Use elements of show biz as light relief from the more serious business. Use it sparingly as an introduction to serious topics.

5. *Last minute recheck* of every detail.

Physical Arrangements

One person and one person only should be in charge of all physical details. He should work from a master checklist. If the meeting is to be held at a hotel or other convention site, a convention manager will provide assistance.

The accompanying checklists are generalized. They need to be adapted, of course, to your own situation.

Sales Meeting Check List

Accommodations

Agreement with hotel before meeting

☐ Approximate number of guest rooms needed, with breakdown on singles, doubles and suites.

☐ Room rates.

☐ Reservations confirmation.

☐ Copies of reservations to those concerned.

☐ Date majority of group arriving.

☐ Date majority of group departing.

☐ Date uncommitted guest rooms are to be released.

☐ Understanding regarding rooms to be assigned to VIPs, special guests, etc.; those to be paid by company and those complimentary by hotel.

☐ Hospitality suites needed.

☐ Check rooms, gratuities, bars, snacks, service time and date.

Check with hotel prior to meeting
- ☐ Floor plans furnished.
- ☐ Correct date and time for each session.
- ☐ Room assigned for each session: rental.
- ☐ Headquarters room.
- ☐ Seating number, seating plan for each session and speakers' tables.
- ☐ Meetings scheduled, staggered for best traffic flow, including elevator service.
- ☐ Staging required – size.
- ☐ Equipment for each session (check against Equipment and Facilities list).
- ☐ Other special requirements *(immediately prior to meeting, check.)*
- ☐ Check room open and staffed.
- ☐ Seating style as ordered.
- ☐ Enough seats for all conferees.
- ☐ Cooling, heating system operating.
- ☐ P.A. system operating; mikes as ordered.
- ☐ Recording equipment operating.
- ☐ Microphones; number, type as ordered.
- ☐ Lectern in place, light operating, gavel, block.
- ☐ Water pitcher, water at lectern.
- ☐ Water pitcher, water, glasses for conferees.
- ☐ Guard service at entrance door.
- ☐ Ash trays, stands, matches.
- ☐ Overhead projector and screen.
- ☐ Teleprompter operating.
- ☐ Pencils, note pads, paper.
- ☐ Chart stands, easels, blackboards, related equipment.
- ☐ Piano, organ, signs, flags, banners.
- ☐ Lighting as ordered.
- ☐ Special flowers, plants as ordered.
- ☐ Any other special facilities.
- ☐ Directional signs if meeting room difficult to locate.
- ☐ If meeting room changed, post notice conspicuously.
- ☐ Stenographer present.
- ☐ Photographer present.
- ☐ Remove organizational property *(assign someone who will after meeting).*
- ☐ Check for forgotten property.

Equipment and Facilities

- ☐ Special notes to be placed in guest boxes.
- ☐ Equipment availability lists and prices furnished.
- ☐ Signs for registration desk, hospitality rooms, members only, tours, welcome.
- ☐ Lighting — spots, floods, operators.
- ☐ Staging — size.
- ☐ Overhead projector and screen.
- ☐ Blackboards, flannel boards, magnetic boards.
- ☐ Chart stands and easels.
- ☐ Lighted lectern, teleprompter, gavel, block.
- ☐ Gavel, block.
- ☐ PA system — microphones, types, number.
- ☐ Recording equipment, operator.
- ☐ Motion picture, filmstrip, or slide projection equipment, blackout switch.
- ☐ Special flowers and plants.
- ☐ Piano (tuned), organ.
- ☐ Phonograph and records.
- ☐ Printed services.
- ☐ Dressing rooms for entertainers.
- ☐ Parking, garage facilities.
- ☐ Decorations — check fire regulations.
- ☐ Special equipment.
- ☐ Agreement on total cost of extra services.
- ☐ Telephones.
- ☐ Photographer.
- ☐ Stenographer.
- ☐ Flags, banners. Hotel furnishes, U. S., Canadian, State flags.
- ☐ Radio and TV broadcasting.
- ☐ Live and engineering charges.
- ☐ Closed-circuit TV.

- ☐ Time and days required.
- ☐ Registration cards; content, number.
- ☐ Tables; number, size.
- ☐ Tables for filling out forms; number, size.
- ☐ Chairs.
- ☐ Ash trays.
- ☐ Typewriters, number, type.
- ☐ Personnel — own or hotel's.
- ☐ Water pitchers, glasses.
- ☐ Lighting.
- ☐ Bulletin boards, number, size.
- ☐ Signs.
- ☐ Notepaper, pens, pencils, sundries.
- ☐ Telephones *(immediately prior to opening, check)*.
- ☐ Personnel, their knowledge of procedure.
- ☐ Information desired on registration cards.
- ☐ Information on badges.
- ☐ Handling of guests, dignitaries.
- ☐ Program, other material in place.
- ☐ Emergency housing.
- ☐ Hospitality desk.
- ☐ Wastebaskets.
- ☐ Mimeograph registration lists.

Speakers

Prior to convention:
- [ ] Have speakers been invited early?
- [ ] Informed on length of time available to them?
- [ ] Informed on type of talk desired? Financial arrangements understood?
- [ ] Fee or expenses only?
- [ ] Fee or fee plus expenses?
- [ ] When is payment to be made?
- [ ] Biographical material and photos available for publicity and introduction?
- [ ] Is speaker's wife coming along?
- [ ] Has hotel reservation been made?
- [ ] Will speaker require special equipment?
- [ ] Has he been furnished with program or tentative program as early as possible?
- [ ] Date majority of group arriving.
- [ ] Is anyone local closely related (personally or businesswise) who should be invited to hear him speak?
- [ ] Has someone been designated to meet speaker upon arrival in city?

Immediately prior to meeting, check:
- [ ] Has speaker been personally introduced to officers and head table? Have special needs been met?
- [ ] Blackboard or easel?
- [ ] Pointers, chalk in place?
- [ ] Need help in turning charts?
- [ ] Projector on hand?
- [ ] Projector stand available?
- [ ] Projectionist on hand?
- [ ] Is material to be passed out?
- [ ] Will he need assistance?

Other important points:
- [ ] Is emergency speaker available in case of a "no-show?"

Decorations:
- ☐ Have decorations and storage space for decorations prior to use been arranged for?
- ☐ In case of elaborate decorations have fire regulations and hotel policy been checked?

Entertainment:
- ☐ Has an interesting entertainment program been planned for men, women, and children?

Guests:
- ☐ Have local dignitaries been invited and acceptance received?
- ☐ Provided with tickets?
- ☐ If expected to speak even briefly, have they been forewarned?
- ☐ Arrangements made to welcome them upon arrival?

Publicity:
- ☐ Has an effective publicity committee been set up?
- ☐ Personally called on city editors, radio and TV program directors?
- ☐ Prepared an integrated attendance-building publicity program?
- ☐ Prepared newsworthy releases?
- ☐ Arrangements for photographs for organization and publicity?

Recording:
- ☐ Have arrangements been made to take minutes of the meeting, to type resolutions, to mimeograph proceedings?

Registration List:
- ☐ Have arrangements been made to mimeograph registration lists?

Sign Check List:
- ☐ Registration Desk, Hospitality Room, Tickets, Information, Members Only, Special Events, Hospitality Committee, Special Tours, Ladies' Committee, No Smoking, Welcome, Advance Registration.

Signs:
- ☐ Have adequate signs been prepared to assure smooth operation, and is masking tape available for mounting?

Notes

Notes

Notes

Post-Meeting Follow-Through

An ancient philosopher once observed that "In deeds — not words — the outcome of the battle lies."

Indeed, the effective meeting is a vital management tool and the successful companies are those who use it for all it is worth.

But it is equally true that action must follow planning or the best plans might just as well not have been formulated. Good intentions are not enough. As the old saw goes, "The road to hell is paved with good intentions."

The meeting is a legitimate management function and as such its effects should be measured. Therefore, a post-meeting follow-up to determine if the meeting decisions have been, or are being carried out, is as important as the success of the meeting itself. If the meeting set a goal, was the goal attained? If, for instance, a national sales meeting is called to direct the salesmen to take up new strategies in the field, are they doing just that? If not, why not?

Think back to some meetings that you attended recently. List some important decisions made, particularly those calling for follow-through by participants. Check off those that accomplished something and those that were failures. You are likely to find a surprising and distressing imbalance between the time invested and the paucity of results.

The simplest single explanation is that we are creatures of habit. Most of us really don't want to change unless we have to. It takes more than a mere decision to get us to discontinue things we have been doing and to take on new ways of life. Any new action decision calls for a double-barreled charge: with one barrel, you must dislodge previous methods; with the other, you must propel new ways into orbit.

How to Fix Accountability

Obviously, there are different aspects of accountability depending upon the type of meeting and the roles played by those who participated. A financial report pinpointing problem areas in the company profit-and-loss picture will present a different type of accountability than that of a highly technical presentation or a sales meeting. The controller is not responsible for a decrease in sales but he is responsible in getting that point clearly across to management. A plant manager may not be responsible for a sharp rise in costs in some area of production but he is accountable to find out why or what is responsible for that rise and then see that the recommendations to correct the situation are carried out.

Fixing accountability means making an action assignment for which one or more people will be held responsible in specific ways. Theoretically, all that you need do is to tell someone his assignment and, as a good organization man, he will automatically follow through. In practice, getting follow-through on meeting decisions usually demands a great deal of effort and ingenuity. This starts with the actual planning of the meeting, even before the decisions are reached.

Who Gets Pinned?

By the time a discussion gets well under way in the meeting room, you should be able to decide who will carry out the anticipated decisions. Of course not all the results of a meeting are decided beforehand, but you ought to be able to anticipate probable outcomes with a degree of accuracy.

One reason you need to make tentative allocations of responsibility is because these color your judgment as to how much of a decision can be made; the decision often hinges on who is available to carry it out and how long it will take him. Therefore, when planning the meeting agenda you might assign some of the discussion to those who are expected to carry out the action.

As discussion progresses during the meeting, and as decisions start to take form, the logical points of follow-up begin to manifest themselves. At this stage, bureaucratic concerns over the distribution of responsibility have to be considered. As a general rule, responsibility is delegated to the head of a functional activity. This is not always clear-cut, particularly when new responsibilities are to be assigned, but if confusion is not settled, participants may go away from the meeting feeling that they have responsibilities which actually were not conferred upon them.

Of course, the logic of functional accountability doesn't always hold up. There are times when a functional head is overloaded with conflicting responsibilities. Occasionally, factors of personality or competence may dictate that special assignments be made outside of the ordinary framework. This may call for adriotness and tact on the part of the meeting chairman.

The Principle of Feedback

The key to a follow-up system is to build in check points requiring progress or accomplishment reports. To pin down the action, then, you must also pin down the elements of feedback.

For example, you might decide that a major presentation is to be made on a date five weeks in the future. Right there in the meeting, you would block out the time needed to organize, prepare, and rehearse for the meeting. The key date is that of the first rehearsal, when all of the participants in the important presentation are to start working together. If this date has been set realistically to allow for slippage and repeat rehearsals, it could then be accepted as the critical feedback date, for adherence to it will probably mean the difference between good and bad follow-through

Depending on the experience with previous such presentations, the chairman might decide that he should have additional feedbacks. For example, he might want some assurance that each participant has completed his own preparatory work. This might call for a check-up meeting at a date which would allow enough time for performance, yet would not result in too much slippage if progress were found to be unsatisfactory.

The organization of the follow-through will depend upon the importance of the action, the number of people involved, the complexity of the undertaking, and the seasoning of the group. On this last point, the meeting chairman has some latitude. If he has already been through a number of similar exercises with the same people, he can confidently lessen feedback requirements.

Another technique in planning follow-through is to apportion the critical responsibilities so that not too many of them fall in any one area or with any one person. This is insurance against illness or catastrophe of any kind.

Although it is important that you do not fragment responsibility for control, you can delegate a certain amount of it without actually giving it up. In fact, under current concepts of project management, when responsibility is given to someone, that person is also responsible for getting action from others upon whom his assignment is dependent. To this extent, action follow-through is decentralized beyond the ordinary responsibility of the meeting chairman. His responsibility is limited to checking on the key action designee — the activity or project leader.

The Minutes of the Meeting

It is amazing how much of what transpires in a meeting is lost forever unless good records are kept. This was dramatized by a memory-retention study of attendees of a psychological society meeting in England. Two weeks after the meeting the attendees were asked to write down what they recalled. The resulting average was only 8.4 per cent of all the points actually covered in the meeting. Forty-two per cent of what they thought they remembered was incorrectly recalled. Many of the items remembered were not even covered at the meeting!

Unless we record things immediately, we begin forgetting about them very, very fast. In the example just cited, the meeting was at least reasonably neutral. In the typical business meeting, there is a fairly high degree of emotional content, conditioned by the desire of the participants to interpret what transpired from the standpoint of their own best interests.

What Goes Into the Minutes

The recall of things that did not transpire could be even greater under such circumstances. The moral of the story is that you must put down the decisions reached at the time they are reached and in a manner which assures that there is no ambiguity as to what actually was decided.

At one extreme of minute-taking, you tape the meeting and transcribe the tape for a word-for-word record of what transpired. Then there can be no argument. Key items of decision, expressed succinctly so that all present can agree or disagree as to what was actually decided, can be entered right on the tape and abstracted later.

Action minutes, for purposes of follow-through, are not a full record of the proceedings, of course. A more extensive summary can be prepared subsequently — verified if necessary — and distributed to all participants and departments. The action minutes, however, should record the very essence of decisions reached and responsibilities assigned. They should not detail the blow-by-blow discussion. While they should be brief, preferably in outline form, they need not be confined to a single page, although this is certainly a desirable objective. It is pointless to obscure meaning in order to be terse.

Participants often request that their positions be recorded. These can go into the regular meeting transcript; they need not go into the action minutes, which are intended to assure that there is no misunderstanding on key decisions.

Very few meetings proceed in an utterly logical manner for the benefit of the note-taker. In the course of a discussion, subsidiary decisions and action assignments might be made. The note-taker might list these on a separate sheet, for his convenience. If, however, he wants these items to appear in sequence, he might put brackets around them, thus distinguishing them as independent items of decision and action calling for some type of follow-through.

On the main topics of discussion, the note-taker should list agreement and disagreement, with some brief explanation of the character of each. Also, he should identify those who line up with the different positions.

Sometimes a discussion will generate ideas that do not in themselves end in any kind of action judgment. If the note-taker senses that the worthiness of these ideas has been recognized, he might also record these in brackets as they came up. Or he might put them on a separate sheet to be turned over to the meeting chairman as an auxiliary extract of the meeting report for such follow-up action as the chairman thinks warranted.

Getting Agreement on Decisions

The chairman himself — possibly with the assistance of his note-taker — should summarize decisions as they are reached. If the meeting is devoted to a single topic, he might do this at the end of the meeting, or he might discuss decisions as they are reached. If a number of topics are brought up during the meeting, the chairman should dispose of each as discussion on it is concluded. To group them at the end of the proceedings would reopen discussion when there is insufficient time to permit this.

This is an opportunity to use the overhead projector. The chairman can write out the decision on a sheet of transparency film and project it right there in the room for all to see. If he wants a neater presentation, he can have this in a few moments by having a secretary type out the decision and make a transparency immediately. If there is any argument over the decisions that are reached, the wording of the material on the transparency can be easily erased, and changed with a grease pencil.

The final version can then be given to the secretary and run through an office copying machine with ordinary copying machine paper to produce copies to hand out to each participant as he leaves the meeting.

The chairman should be most careful in testing the clarity of understanding on the points in greatest controversy. These are the actual or potential friction points, identified by expressions of misgivings, at the very least. These sensitive areas not only require assurance of clarity, but should suggest to the chairman critical control points for purposes of follow-up.

Follow-Ups After the Meeting

In some cases, particularly with his own employees, the chairman may want to hold private meeting follow-ups. He may want to go into aspects of the action with individual employees which might involve embarrassment if taken up in front of all participants.

No later than two or three days after the meeting, the chairman should send out the regular minutes which should include and elaborate upon the action minutes distributed at the time of the meeting. This can be used by the chairman as an excuse for underscoring pending actions of any kind.

The effective meeting chairman will use the telephone anywhere from a few days to a week after the meeting to assure proper action has been initiated.

One might question why we have so much preoccupation in this chapter with pinning down understanding and with subsequent follow-up.

This preoccupation should not be regarded as a matter of distrust. Rather, the astute meeting chairman must recognize that people are fallible. They forget. They tend to interpret from their own naturally prejudiced standpoints. They tend also to let new actions slide when they are subject to normal workload pressures.

The effective meeting chairman leaves nothing to chance.

Summing Up

The purpose of this book is to underscore the importance of meetings as a vital management tool. As companies grow and responsibility is proliferated, decisions become the province of group thinking, rather than the automatic expression of the will of a single executive. Meetings are here to stay and the wise manager knows that he must make the best possible use of them in order to justify the expenditure of manpower diverted from the front lines to the meeting table. Growing companies can achieve an important by-product when their meetings are well planned and executed. This is the training of future executives. It is hoped that this book will help managers, present and future, to become more effective meeting leaders.

Notes

APPENDIX

The Art of a Good Visual

Elegance of language may not be in the power of all of us, but simplicity and straightforwardness are–Alford.

Another writer noted that simplicity is the first step of Nature and the last step of Art.

Simplicity of expression lies at the root of effective communication. Similarly, simplicity of the *means* by which we get things done and communicate to others can only be viewed in highest esteem. Think of the simplicity of the common wheel and yet the enormous impact it has had on civilization.

Similarly, one of the primary characteristics associated with the use of the overhead projector is simplicity. Simplicity in the making of visual aids and simplicity in showing them. This combination provides an effective communications system that can be used successfully by anyone.

No one holds an exclusive franchise on creativity. And while it may not be in the realm of possibility for all, either by birthright, technical training, circumstance or the wherewithal to produce Hollywood type audio-visual spectaculars, it is within the reach of almost everyone to produce effective visual aids quickly, easily and inexpensively, right in their own office.

Overhead projection transparencies have special merit. Only two pieces of equipment are necessary. One to copy. One to project.

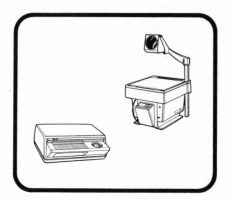

Visual No. 1

A finished transparency can be made from printed or drawn material in a matter of seconds. There is no costly or time-consuming processing involved. They can be projected with the flick of a switch. Neat. Clean. Quick. Graphic. Inexpensive.

In addition, they enable a secretary or a time-pressed executive to experience the satisfaction of individual creativity. For many, they may be a refreshingly welcome change of pace from routine business work, while at the same time performing the vital business function of effective communication.

From the viewpoint of the secretary it offers the opportunity for personal creativity and the chance to be of increased value to those for whom she works. While the art of excellent speechmaking is not within the grasp of everyone, the creation of good visual aids by the secretary can be learned easily. And they can be the very assist which will give the poise and self confidence necessary for making an effective presentation.

They also can be instrumental in overcoming the language barrier which exists from one occupation to another.

Most people do not recognize that we all speak different versions of our native language because of the materials, ideas and methods we use to accomplish the tasks in our particular fields of endeavor. It might be said that we all have different dialects just as the Chinese all speak the same language but in different dialects from one province to another.

The physician, comptroller, engineer, production supervisor, etc., all use words and phrases foreign to each other. Even within one field a language barrier may exist. Two neuro-surgeons may carry on a conversation that a pediatrician cannot understand. An advertising man in an organization will use different terminology to describe elements of his work than would a lab technician in the same company. An engineer in a business firm uses a different language than his colleague in the marketing department.

All of this poses the problem of language barrier, and therefore a communications barrier, in the business meeting. The use of language foreign or not completely understandable to others results in misunderstanding, misdirected efforts, lost time and costly mistakes.

A good visual used to illustrate an idea or plan can help solve this problem of communication. It can provide an effective tool for an executive in the meeting room, no matter what particular language he uses in his particular occupation.

Visual No. 2

Visual No. 3

Elements of a good visual

The art of creating a good visual is simply a matter of keeping a few basic principles in mind. To convey these to you, I will present them as though I were addressing you in person, using a script and a series of visuals.

Script

First of all, let us always keep
in mind the function of a visual.
It is meant to assist communication.
To make clear, reinforce and supplement spoken material. To combine visual material with audio material for great memory retention and impact.
It is not meant to take the place of spoken material, nor detract from it.

There are three basic elements contained in a good visual.

1. Visibility.
2. Simplicity.
3. Clarity.

Let's take them one at a time.

Visibility.

It's obvious that a visual must be visible to all—even to those farthest from the screen. This requires that the image size be proportionate to the size of the transparency. Lettering should be at least ¼ of an inch high, and legible. One rule of thumb says that "the smallest image seen on the screen should be one inch high for every 30 feet of viewing distance."

Another states that if the material is readable with the naked eye at 10 feet, the transparency will have adequate visibility.

Presenter's Notes

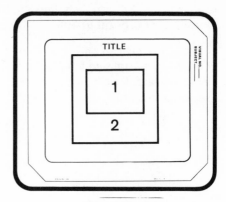

Visual No. 4

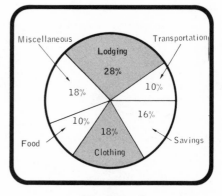

Visual No. 5

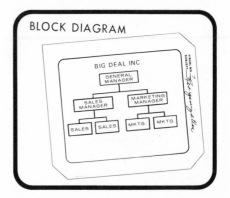

Visual No. 6

Printed matter on the transparency should be no closer than ⅜ inch from any edge.

Visuals should be shown horizontally, when possible. They appear larger and conform to the images shown on televison and movie screens to which most people are accustomed.

Material should be positioned *near the top* of the visual if possible to assure maximum visibility to those farthest from the screen.

Space should be left, when desired, for adding information during the course of the presentation.

The use of color or shading on transparencies will not only add visibility but it permits variety, emphasis on priority materials, isolation of prominent data—and adds pleasure to the beholder.

Simplicity

Simplicity, simplicity, simplicity. Remember that a good visual is meant to aid, to supplement and reinforce spoken material, not to take its place, detract from it, nor overwhelm it.

The human eye can accept and retain only so much at one time. A good visual will depict only one idea at a time.

The flame begins about 1/8 inch above the top of the candle[25] and at its base the flame has a blue tint[27]. Immediately around the wick in a region about 1/4 inch wide and extending about 1/2 inch above the top of the wick[28] the flame is dark[29]. This dark region is roughly conical in shape[30]. Around this zone and extending about half an inch above the dark zone is a region which emits yellow light[31], bright but not blinding[32]. The flame has rather sharply defined sides[33], but a ragged top[34]. The wick is white where it emerges from the candle[35], but from the base of the flame to the end of the wick[36] it is black, appearing burnt, except for the last 1/16 inch[37] where it glows red[38]. The wick curls over about 1/4 inch from its end[39]. As the candle becomes shorter, the wick shortens too, so as to extend roughly a constant length above the top of the candle[40]. Heat is emitted by the flame[41], enough so that it becomes uncomfortable in ten or twenty seconds if one holds his finger 1/4 inch to the side of the quiet flame[41] or three or four inches above the flame[42].

The top of a quietly burning candle becomes wet with a colorless liquid[43] and becomes bowl shaped[44]. If the flame is blown, one side of this bowl-shaped top may become liquid, and the liquid trapped in the bowl may drain down the candle's side[45]. As it courses down, the colorless liquid cools[46], becomes translucent[47], and gradually solidifies from the outside[48], attaching itself to the side of the candle[49]. In the absence of a draft, the candle can burn for hours without such dripping[50]. Under these conditions, a stable pool of clear liquid remains in the bowl-shaped top of the candle[51]. The liquid rises slightly around the wick[52], wetting the base of the wick as high as the base of the flame[53].

Visual No. 7

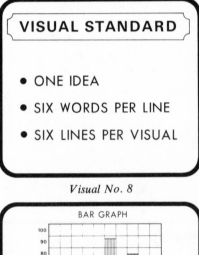

Visual No. 8

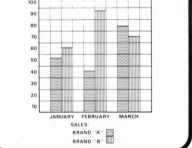

Visual No. 9

Do not try to cram too much information into one visual. Limit it to essential information. Avoid secondary information or too much primary information. Here is an example of a cluttered visual. It contains far too much information.

The less copy, the better. Limit information on each visual to six words per line, six lines per visual . . . and no more than two illustrations per visual.

Clarity.

The meaning of a good visual will be immediately clear to all who see it.

A good visual will be legible, vivid, understandable. It will get, and hold, attention.

A good visual will have a clearly defined objective. It will be consistent with the material spoken by the speaker and represent, reinforce or picture the nub of the idea he is trying to get across.

Remember that people are accustomed to reading material from left

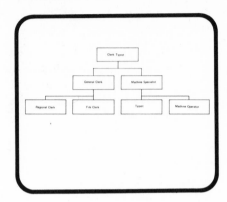

Visual No. 10

Visual No. 11

Visual No. 12

to right and from top to bottom. Your visual should be arranged with that pattern in mind.

This is an example of a good visual depicting Clarity.

This is not.

Speaker Control.

A speaker who does not have control over his visual materials, and his audience, is in the awkward position of the dog being wagged by his tail.

One of the distinct advantages of overhead projection is that it's simplicity and flexibility of operation permits a maximum amount of speaker control.

He may turn the projection on or off, as he chooses, without having to rely on a second person.

He may remove information, or add it at will.

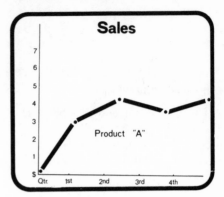

Visual No. 12a

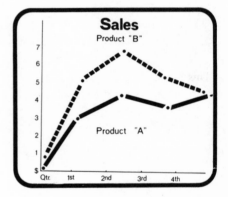

Visual No. 12b

He may start out with one basic transparency,

then reveal additional information by placing a second transparency over the first.

Even so, the speaker has enough to do in maintaining interest and attention with his audience without being distracted or disrupted by badly arranged or disorganized visual materials and equipment.

His visual materials should be placed in logical sequence and marked legibly so that he may find and refer back to them at a moment's notice.

Marking pens or other writing tools should be readily available with which to add or delete information.

The equipment should be checked for good operating condition beforehand. Lenses and lights should be cleaned to assure maximum visibility and clarity.

In sum, the mechanics of making the presentation should be as well organized as the presentation itself.

Lettering — The Styles, Sizes and Techniques

The quality of a transparency can hinge on the lettering it contains. Carelessly drawn letters can detract from the cleanest, most attractive design. And, conversely, neatly lettered and organized transparencies can be attractive even when they lack illustration.
There are several easy ways to letter neatly . . .

Typing

Most electric typewriters do not provide neat. readable lettering for

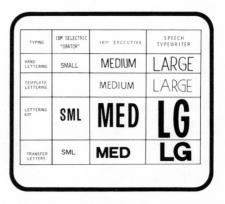

Visual No. 13

your transparencies. However, IBM typewriters are excellent for this job.

We suggest that you type in *capitals only*; some small letters tend to fill in during the transparency-making process.

And whenever possible, avoid manual typewriters. Even the best typists hit different letters with varying pressures . . . and the resulting unevenness tends to be exaggerated when projected.

Tracing and Stenciling

Select the lettering size and style you want and trace it onto your original. Nothing to it. But exercise care and use a sharp pen or pencil.

Lettering templates for making stenciled letters are available in most stationery supply stores.

Freehand

Not as difficult as many people think. Use the lines of the grids in your Speech Forms to keep your letters even.

Pre-Set Type

Sometimes the words you need can be found in a newspaper or a magazine—printed and ready to clip and fix to your original.

If you can find the words, use them. Such type is usually neat and properly spaced for easy reading.

Custom Types

Recently, small phototype and other "cold" type producing machines have been introduced in offices and school art departments. This equipment, like the popular VariTyper machine, produces words on paper strips which may be trimmed and pasted to your original.

Transfer Letters

Transfer letters make it possible to add information to a finished transparency. These transparent, colored letters may be applied directly to the front surface of the prepared transparency by laying the lettering sheet face down and rubbing the back of the sheet with a blunt pencil or some other smooth, rounded instrument.

Visual No. 14

Suggested Comments and Order of Presentation

Illustrations

Good illustrations can take several forms. They may be diagrams or simple charts, for instance, as well as pictures. But remember, whatever the illustration you choose, keep it simple . . . as few lines as possible, and no more than one or two drawings to a transparency.

Magazines, Texts, Published Reports

If you can find the illustration you need in any of these sources, clip it and fix it to your original. (Paste down on the top of the illustration, leaving the remainder loose during the transparency-making process.)

The considerations here are size and quality. Obviously any illustration too large for the "live" area of the transparency should be eliminated. Quality, in this case, means clarity of line and sharpness of detail. Again, magnification will exaggerate flaws.

Tracing

The same rules apply to tracing illustrations that were covered in tracing as a lettering technique: care and the use of a sharp pencil or pen.

Clip Art

There are several prepared art services available through most of the art store and stationery supply centers. They include drawings categorized by subject—people, transportation, animals, etc.

The quality is usually excellent. These illustration services are usually sold on a subscription basis . . . to advertising companies, art houses and newspapers. You may find them in the art department at your company.

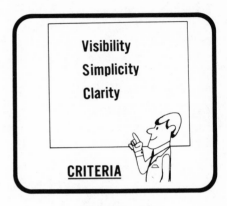

Visual No. 15

Suggested Comments and Order of Presentation

In summary, let me say that the overhead projection transparency system is one of the best of the visual media because it combines simplicity of use and simplicity in making visuals. This powerful combination provides the opportunity for creative visual communication for everyone, right in their own offices, quickly, graphically and inexpensively. It provides the secretary, not only the opportunity to be personally creative, but to be of greatly increased value to those for whom she works. Her mastery of the art of a good visual will provide her boss with the poise, confidence and resources necessary for an effective presentation.
But remember to follow these three guidelines for a good visual:
1. Visibility.
2. Simplicity.
3. Clarity.

Notes

ABOUT THE AUTHOR

The author of *How to Run Better Business Meetings* can lay claim to 25 years of involvement in his subject. Since coming to 3M Company in 1946, Bert Auger has been involved one way or another in thousands of business meetings. A large share of these took place in hotels and motels throughout the country.

He is well aware of the role of the business meeting as an essential part of modern business management. The techniques that produce good meetings have long been of special interest. He is familiar with the theory and the practice.

A key individual behind the success of 3M's Visual Products Division from its inception as a small research group just over a decade ago, Mr. Auger well understands the total significance of business meetings. The success of this venture at 3M is dependent upon solving the problems of group communications both in industry and in education.

This book is only part of Mr. Auger's involvement in writing and publishing. He also is responsible for and manages 3M's various activities in publishing which now includes curriculum materials and publications.

Mr. Auger is by training a chemist. He graduated from the University of Michigan in 1946. His war service was with the Air Force as a navigator on a B17 in Italy. At 3M he started as a chemist and held the post of technical director in two divisions before his present assignment as General Manager of the Visual Products Division. An around-the-clock executive, he devotes what spare time he has to family activities at his lakeside home in St. Paul. He is married and has three children. A little golf, boating and reading are his principal pastimes. History is of special interest.